Francis C. Sessions

On the Wing through Europe

Francis C. Sessions

On the Wing through Europe

ISBN/EAN: 9783744757867

Printed in Europe, USA, Canada, Australia, Japan

Cover: Foto ©Andreas Hilbeck / pixelio.de

More available books at **www.hansebooks.com**

ON THE WING THROUGH EUROPE.

ON THE WING

THROUGH EUROPE.

BY A
BUSINESS MAN.

COLUMBUS, OHIO:
H. W. DERBY & CO.

Copyright, 1880, by
F. C. SESSIONS.

Press of Francis Hart & Co. New-York.

Dedication.

✠

I Dedicate this Book to my dear Wife,

Mary,

A good woman and true,
Whose noble and self-sacrificing spirit opened the way
For her husband to travel abroad for a few delightful months,
For rest and recuperation greatly needed,
Cheerfully taking upon herself
All the cares and responsibilities of home,
That he might be benefited and
Made happy.

CONTENTS.

LETTER I.   PAGE 1.

Across the Deep.... Queenstown, Cork, and Blarney Castle....
An Irish Cattle Fair.... How the Irish Peasant Lives....
Lakes of Killarney.

LETTER II.   PAGE 18.

Parting Glimpses of the Emerald Isle.... Cathedral Restoration... Welsh Scenery... Llanberis... Snowdon... Chester Cathedral.... Eaton Hall.... The Hotels.... Railways.

LETTER III.   PAGE 35.

The English Lakes and Homes of the Poets..... Ayr and Robert Burns.... Glasgow: Its Working People, Open Air Services on Sunday, the Old Cathedral.... Ship-yards on the Clyde.... Inverness.... Glencoe.... Loch Ness.

LETTER IV.   PAGE 52.

Visit to the Hebrides.... The Tradition of "Lady Rock"....
Castle of the "Lord of the Isles".... Fingal's Cave....
Iona and Saint Columba.... Reflections.

Contents.

Letter V. Page 63.

The Trossachs....Perth....Edinburgh....Melrose Abbey....York and its Cathedral....Cambridge and its University....Notes and Incidents.

Letter VI. Page 80.

First View of London....The American Minister....Westminster Abbey and Tombs of the Poets....Houses of Parliament and Buckingham Palace....English Equipages and Public Parks.

Letter VII. Page 84.

London Tower....Kew Gardens....The National Gallery....A Royal Display and Garden Fête....The Queen's Stables....The London Slums....The Pulpit Orators of London....Curiosities at Kensington Museum....Environs of London....Royal Academy....Bank of England.

Letter VIII. Page 105.

Eminent British Divines *....Punshon....Pulsford....Wilberforce.

Letter IX. Page 119.

Dr. Joseph Parker....Dr. John Cumming....Canon Farrar....Dean Stanley....Charles H. Spurgeon.

Letter X. Page 135.

From London to Paris....First Impressions of the French Metropolis....The Second Great Exposition....The Tuileries, the Trocadero, and Surroundings....America's Educational Exhibit....Columbus in the Great Exposition.

Letter XI. Page 149.

Fine Art Department of the Exposition....Notable Works by American Artists....Art as an Educator....Paris and Philadelphia....Hotel Life....The French Sabbath.

Letter XII. Page 157.

From Paris to Lucerne....Lake of the Four Forest Cantons....Ascent of the Rigi; Scenes at Sunset and Sunrise; the Ranz des Vaches....Flüelen....Home of Tell....St. Gothard Pass....Glacier du Rhone....The Hanseck.... Sunday at Interlaken.

Letter XIII. Page 174.

Description of the Swiss Capital....Geneva and its Historic Associations....Lovely Lake Leman....The Vale of Chamouni....Mer de Glace....Over the Simplon Pass.... Farewell to Switzerland.

Letter XIV. Page 184.

Sunny Italy....Lago Maggiore and the Borromean Islands.... Milan and its Cathedral....The City of Palaces....Monument to Columbus....Pisa: the Campo Santo, Duomo and Leaning Tower....Rome: Festival of the Assumption of the Virgin: St. Peter's, the Vatican, and their Art Treasures.

Letter XV. Page 199.

Reminiscences of Rome....The Coliseum.....Ancient Baths and Catacombs....The Quirinal....Bay and City of Naples ... Ascent of Vesuvius....Pompeii and its Wonders....Off for New Scenes.

Letter XVI.   Page 214.

Florence, the City of Palaces....The Duomo and Campanile.....Art Collections at the Uffizzi Palace....The Studio of Powers...."The Bride of the Sea."....A Gondola Trip through Venice....Palace of the Doges, San Marco and Clock Tower....Piazza of St. Mark....Evening Recreations.

Letter XVII.   Page 226.

The Old Amphitheater at Verona....Departure from Italy....Trent....German Homelikeness....Munich....The Pinakothek....Famous Americans in Bronze....The Great Breweries....Use of Stimulants....A Novel Species of Morgue....Famous Cemeteries of Europe....Heidelberg and its Students.

Letter XVIII.   Page 240.

Degradation of the Female Peasantry on the Continent....A Sunday in Heidelberg....The Old Castle and the University....A Land of Plenty....Frankfort-on-the-Main....The Judengasse....Antiquities of the City....Down the Rhine....Cologne and its Cathedral.....Thoughts upon Art.

Letter XIX.   Page 253.

Amsterdam: its External Features, Industries, Galleries of Art and Banking Houses....Haarlem and its Flower Gardens....Leyden and the "Pilgrim Fathers"....Royal Marriage Fête at the Hague....Antwerp: its Cathedral and Art Treasures....Brussels: its Hotel de Ville, Lace-makers and Milk-carriers....Return to Paris....Our Representatives Abroad.

LETTER XX.   PAGE 273.

Paris Workingmen....Their Social Character... Peculiarities of Domestic Life... National Faults and their Origin.... Sunday as a Holiday....Musical Societies; their Popularity and Management.

LETTER XXI.   PAGE 281.

Stratford-upon-Avon....Shakespeare's House....Relics of the Poet still existing....Tomb and Epitaph in the Church of the Holy Trinity.

LETTER XXII.   PAGE 290.

Conclusion: On the Atlantic....Thoughts of Home.

APPENDIX.   PAGE 298.

Letter from a Niece of Robert Burns.....An Unpublished Letter of the Poet.

LIST OF ILLUSTRATIONS.

Letter		Page
I.	{ Blarney Castle....Irish Jaunting-car....	8
	{ Lake of Killarney........................	15
II.	....Old Palace, or Derby House, Chester....	27
III.	....Home of Wordsworth, Rydal Mount.....	36
IV.	....Iona Cathedral........................	57
VI.	....Westminster Abbey....................	81
VII.	...Houses of Parliament..................	82
IX.	{ Dean Stanley............................	125
	{ Rev. C. H. Spurgeon.....................	129
X.	...The Trocadero.........................	140
XII.	....Summit of the Rigi....Vitznau..........	161
XIII.	....Crossing the Mer de Glace.............	180
XIV.	....Milan Cathedral.......................	186
XV.	....Bay of Naples and Vesuvius............	204
XVI.	....St. Mark's Place, Venice...............	220
XVIII.	....Heidelberg Castle.....................	242
XIX.	....Milk Vender at Brussels................	265
XXI.	...Shakespeare's Birthplace................	285

PREFACE.

At the unanimous request of the Young Men's Christian Association of this city, given in the cordial and friendly letter printed below, the writer was induced to prepare this account of his visit to the Old World. For the long delay in responding to their most complimentary request, he can only say most frankly that other pressing avocations have hitherto barred the way to a task which he has now gladly endeavored to fulfill:

F. C. SESSIONS, ESQ.:

DEAR SIR:— We have been directed by the Young Men's Christian Association, of this city, to request you to prepare and arrange for publication the result of your observations and experiences in your recent travels in Europe.

Your letters to the press while absent attracted very general attention, and lead us to believe that they are *worthy to be put in a more extended and permanent form. The Association will cheerfully accept a book in such form as your judgment and taste shall dictate, and assume the responsibility of such a circulation in this and other cities as we are confident it will merit.*

Permit us to assure you that we not only express a unanimous wish of the Association, but also that of a wide circle of friends.

Fraternally yours,
GEO. H. TWISS,
W. Y. MILES.
Committee of Y. M. C. A.
WM. G. DUNN, *President.*
Columbus, Ohio, November, 1878.

MESSRS. GEO. H. TWISS AND W. Y. MILES:

GENTLEMEN :—*Allow me to thank you for the kind and flattering request of the Young Men's Christian Association to prepare for publication the result of my observations during my European tour. As soon as my pressing business demands will admit, I will endeavor to comply with your wishes,—not because I am vain enough to believe that my book will possess anything deserving a place among the valuable works written by professional men traversing the same* ground, but more with the hope of aiding financially so valuable and worthy an association, which is doing so much for the young men of our city, in whose welfare I feel so deep an interest. It is this that induces me to venture before the public, regardless of criticism. A book of travels by a business man will at least be a novelty, and may attract the attention of business men.

FRANCIS C. SESSIONS.

I take with pleasure this opportunity to acknowledge my great indebtedness to my pastor, Rev. R. G. Hutchins, D. D., of the First Congregational Church of this city, the genial companion of my travels. The experience of Dr. Hutchins as a traveler abroad, his intelligent mapping-out of our route, and the friendly interest he manifested in endeavoring to have me see all that was most noteworthy, afforded me not only great pleasure and content, but also furnished opportunities of really enjoying the utmost possible in the somewhat limited period of our tour. Always happy and joyful himself, he made this journey to me equally pleasant and instructive, and the memory of it will remain, like all things of beauty, "a joy forever."

And here let me add one further word of acknowledgment in regard to his two interesting letters on "Eminent English Divines," which give, I cannot but feel, a greater value to my work, and which, I am sure, my readers will peruse with a pleasure equal to my own.

I am also greatly indebted to Mr. William M. Briggs, of New York, for the taste and discretion shown in supervising this little work while in process of publication.

INTRODUCTION.

THE letters contained in this volume were written hastily for the *Daily Ohio State Journal*, of Columbus, as I could catch a moment's time on the cars, or while stopping for rest during the intervals of travel and sight-seeing. I had no expectation that they would be received with so much favor, and I cannot but think that the words of appreciation so often addressed to me come from over-partial friends, and that, on the other hand, I have not heard the criticisms of those less favorably impressed.

It has often occurred to me that many, while traveling abroad, do not derive that instruction and entertainment which they might, and fail to have their interest sufficiently awakened in the novel and lovely scenes through which they are passing, because they have not, by previous preparation, informed themselves of the countries and peoples which they were to visit. Thus, not properly prepared either to appreciate or understand them, they consequently bring back, when they return, but little beyond a mere collection of isolated facts and inadequate impressions of all that should have enriched their future lives, to the benefit of themselves and of their friends. Nothing, it appears to me, can impart such healthy vigor to body and mind, through agreeable exercise and continuous change of scene, as travel; and nothing, perhaps, within the range of moderate expenditure, can confer so rich a fund of knowledge to the intelligent observer as the conclusions deduced from a personal and faithful study of the governments, manners, customs and institutions of the peoples visited.

An American needs to learn that his countrymen do not monopolize all the intelligence and enterprise of the world; but still, as a close observer, he may honestly return, notwithstanding the many novel and excellent usages he encounters abroad, with a greater admiration of his own country and its republican government and institutions, where every man, be he ever so poor, has an opportunity to rise to opulence and influence, according as he makes himself their rightful possessor through industry, education, and earnestness and honesty of purpose. Too often Americans are overweening in their national pride, and imagine that they have nothing to learn from the mother-land; but they should remember that her great age and experience count something in the scale, and that at least we can there gather what things are best, and what things safest to avoid. Moreover, they should never forget that we have an interest and common stock in the literature and science which come to us from our transatlantic ancestors, and that we are naturally affiliated to them in all noble efforts and aspirations.

I have tried to give in my letters life-like pictures and various reflections upon what I saw abroad; these may seem commonplace, perhaps, to older travelers, but my excuse may be pleaded in a remark made by a certain friend, viz.: "Your letters contain observations upon common matters which most travelers omit,"—which, indeed, I hope may prove true.

Many there are who, in traveling abroad, have some special object in view in which they are wholly absorbed, and which almost exclusively occupies their letters, but fails to interest the general reader, leaving him uninformed upon those common points which are of the most pertinent interest, and about which almost every one wishes to know. Trusting that the perusal of this volume may supply information perhaps often found wanting in works of more pretentious effort, and hoping it may prove a pleasure to the reader, as its writing was to the author, —a happy record of rare enjoyment amid novel scenes in those lands from which we or our ancestors came,—I submit it to the friends who have requested it, and to such others as may read it, with confidence that those critically disposed will remember that it was written with the earnest purpose of conveying genuine impressions, and that it is not assumed to be altogether free from faults and minor errors. F. C. S.

ON THE WING THROUGH EUROPE.

I.

ACROSS THE DEEP....QUEENSTOWN, CORK AND BLARNEY CASTLE....AN IRISH CATTLE FAIR....HOW THE IRISH PEASANT LIVES....LAKES OF KILLARNEY.

Glengariff, Ireland.

IT has been the dream of my life to visit the Old World. Everybody does so nowadays. "Going to Europe?" says a friend, "truly, it is not much of an event now." We were only eight days in crossing the ocean in the *City of Berlin*, a splendid floating palace five hundred and twenty-five feet long by forty-five feet beam, and thirty-six feet deep, indicating five hundred horse-power, and steaming sixteen knots an hour. She is the largest steamship afloat, except the *Great Eastern*, and is nearly as long as the distance from Broad to State Street in front of our Ohio State House, at Columbus—the latest and most commodious form of ocean traveling to be found; she is supplied with steam by twelve boilers, which are heated by thirty-six furnaces, ample means being adopted to insure ventilation in the furnace-room, and, indeed, in every part of the vessel, and the boilers are so arranged that any of them can be cut off. There are accommodations for seventeen hundred passengers, and a crew of one hundred and fifty. She is a naval mansion. In our state-room, which is eight and a half feet long, the same measure in width, and seven feet four inches high, are a sofa and two berths. While conversing with an officer in regard to the excellent arrangements for washing, he informed me that there are between three and four miles of lead-pipe in the vessel. We had a smooth sea all the way over except the first day, when nearly every one was sick. I asked a sailor, "Do you call this a smooth sea or a rough one?" He replied: "Smooth—only a nasty swell," which we were all realizing. I lost only one meal during the entire voyage, and consequently found it delightful. Every morning a salt-water bath, in marble bath-rooms, supplied with hot and cold water, could be enjoyed; whilst the eating and drinking—in fact the entire *menu*—was all that a hungry voyager could desire. One of the pleasures on board was to examine the novelties of the ship, and promenade the long upper and lower decks.

There were passengers from all parts of the world, many of our own States being represented—Ohio sending in her quota from Cincinnati, Springfield, Dayton, Cleveland and Columbus. Doctors of divinity, doctors of the law and of medicine, presidents and professors of colleges with their families, men of business, lawyers—indeed every class was there present. Various amusements filled up the leisure hours—lectures, concerts, reading and recitations, quoits, shovelboard, chess (and too much card-playing). Dr. Gregory, President of Illinois University, read a paper on "Antagonism of Labor and Capital," and Mrs. Lippincott (Grace Greenwood) recited admirably several pieces, and her only daughter sang Scotch and French ballads in a voice whose sweetness delighted all. She is going to London to cultivate her musical talent, which already gives indication of a successful future. We have a promise that at some coming time both mother and daughter will visit Columbus, and furnish us an opportunity for enjoying their charming readings, recitations and music. Mrs. Lippincott remembers her former visits to our capital with pleasure. With hair just flecked with gray, and with her large black eyes intelligent as ever, she seems hardly to have grown older. She has the same depreciation of herself, as one never having accomplished anything in the world on account of having been obliged always to write for a living, seeming to forget her ardent labors in behalf of all good moral causes—antislavery, temperance and others. In her recitations and readings she seems to have laid aside the elocutionist, and appears natural and easy.

We started from New York with three other steamships, so that the scene down the bay was an exciting one; but, soon leaving them out of sight, we sped on our voyage, and arrived in just eight days at Queenstown. The days of most anxiety were those in which the dense fogs off the banks of New Foundland enshrouded the ship in impenetrable mist. For parts of two days and nights the fog-whistle was blown every few minutes, and at times I would awake, the whistle impressing me for the moment that we were just sweeping into some station on a sleeping-car, but soon enough I would realize that we were in the midst of the troubled deep. A clergyman, being called upon to preach on board, talked a great deal about the dangers of the sea. The waves were dashing wildly against the ship, and he said that "there was only a thin board between us and eternity." At this the steward exclaimed, quickly: "Thank God, it is a thick plank!" He uttered a sentiment that acccomplished more good than the former.

As we approach land, how our hearts thrill at the first sight of that Old World of history and long renown, so different in every respect from the New. We first see the headlands and mountains of Kerry, on the extreme south-westerly point of Ireland, between Bantry Bay on the south and Kenmare Bay on the north. Probably more voyagers from the western world have greeted Europe at these little points of view than in any other locality. Our vessel was met by a steam-tender, and the passengers who intended to land for Ireland were, with the European mails, transferred to the latter, which steamed up the beautiful harbor to Queenstown—formerly the old "Cove of Cork," but whose present name is in honor of the Queen's visit, made some fifteen or twenty years ago. The city lies at the west of the harbor on a side-hill, and as we approach it from the ocean, with a bright sun shining upon it, with the shipping around us in every direction, we exclaim, "What a picturesque, beautiful view!" and we feel well prepared to enjoy it after our ocean sail. The beautiful River Lee sweeps round behind it, south-westwardly, to the city of Cork, about twelve miles distant. Here we remained overnight, and attended Sabbath evening service at a small Methodist church, where we heard the congregation sing the same hymns and offer prayers as at home. Doctor H———s made a few remarks on the oneness and fellowship of all followers of Christ, while bringing to them the greetings of Christians in America.

Here we begin to notice the high, thick walls around the residences of the rich, with entrances locked—" where the rich are fenced in and the poor out." Our sail the next morning up the River Lee, in a little open steamer, was one of the most enchanting of my life. On either side the hills are dotted with beautiful dwellings which are surrounded by dense foliage, and every little while one is surprised by the glimpse of some fine architectural villa peeping through the trees. We passed Black Rock, whence William Penn, driven out of England, emigrated to America. Also, we saw a minaret or tower, erected in honor of the kind reception given to Father Mathew by Americans. I had the pleasure of meeting on the boat an intelligent Irish merchant from Cork, who gave me much information about the country, and pointed out the objects of interest. Most of these beautiful homes are occupied by the wealthy merchants and retired citizens of Cork. He said our manufactures were intruding greatly on their own. For instance, leather was formerly one of the chief manufactures of Cork, but latterly has been driven out of market by American leather, which was sold at eighteen cents a pound, while they could not make it for less than twenty-two cents. Also, that by our improvements in machinery, our boots and shoes were sold cheaper in Cork than they themselves could afford to make them: our calicoes and agricultural implements, too, competed successfully with theirs. He deprecated a war with Russia, because the increased taxation caused by it would be that "last straw that breaks the camel's back," as the margin was already so small between the cost of manufactured articles and the prices they fetch, that we Americans would have increased advantage in other things also over their own manufactures.

Cork is a beautiful city, the second in size and trade to Dublin. Here we first met the Irish jaunting-car. Vehicles drawn by horses are here called cars, while what we call cars are known as coaches. This jaunting-car was a great curiosity to us. It is a two-wheeled vehicle, with seats for two each side, back to back, to balance the driver in front, and once started, off we go like Jehu! If one could only be introduced into our city streets everybody would stop to gaze at it.

Our jaunting-car driver was a real Irish wit, who made our journey interesting by his lively sallies, and it seemed indeed as if he had kissed the Blarney Stone, from his surprising facility of speech, accompanied by a good-humor quite equal to his glibness. We asked him, when we saw a large number of women going bare-footed to the fair, "What kind of shoes have those women got on?" Quick as a flash he replied, "They are made of *bare* skin, sir." All through Ireland we found the guides full of wit and ready at repartee, intelligent and willing to give information. I

believe no other nation equal to them in natural fluency of speech.

Our first ride, of course, must be to Blarney Castle, five or six miles distant. The road leading thither out of Cork is a beautiful one, adorned with fine residences, whose grounds are covered with oak, birch, holly and yew trees; with vines and hedges of holly; with myrtle, laurestinus and English ivy; indeed, everywhere we can now see why Ireland is called the "Ever-Green Isle." All the farms look like little garden-spots, separated by hedges, or walls covered with vines. Blarney Castle is a grand old ruin, with the donjon-keep still more than one hundred feet in the air, much better preserved than most ruins; it is said to have been originally the home of the royal McCarthys. The original "Blarney Stone" hangs near the top of the southern wall, and "only fools risk their necks in trying to kiss it." It is claimed by the Irish that any one who kisses it has the gift of eloquence given them. A bright English girl at the hotel told me that it would do just as well to kiss any one that had already kissed it; but that she had *not* kissed it. Of course I did not try to kiss the Blarney Stone, if such were the fact. When we arrived at the

Castle we found flags flying from every eminence, and poles all about, with banners bearing the coat-of-arms of Sir George Colehurst (who owns the three thousand acres upon which the Castle is situated), on account of the marriage which was to take place that day in London of his daughter Julia and Mr. Bruce, of Belfast. All the inhabitants of Blarney were out in their best clothes, as this was a holiday, and a grand *fête* was given, with a dinner free to all, and dancing, with music furnished by the Dutch band from Cork. The table was spread with substantial viands, tastefully arranged among flowers, vines and mottoes. One motto in Irish was "*Cead mille failthe*" (one hundred thousand welcomes); another motto in vines bore the legend, "Long live the happy pair." Here we saw the stables of the owner, and his vehicles, which they called the drag, the brake, the dog-cart, and the barouche—all heavy and cumbersome looking, and not at all like our light, handsome, artistic carriages.

On our return we visited the Cork County Annual Fair, where we had a good opportunity to see the genuine Irish peasant. The men were all well dressed and well shod; but the women, although they wore clean, short woolen dresses, were bare-legged and without shoes. The horses, sheep, and cattle were like stock in Ohio, except that the latter were a short-horned breed, and much smaller than ours. The little donkeys were a great curiosity, and we saw them everywhere, hitched to drays and carts; and how they could draw such loads was a wonder to us—they being about the size of the smallest Shetland ponies. Common cows—small ones—brought eighty dollars; horses, ditto, one hundred and fifty dollars; good, fat lambs, twelve dollars; sheep, eighteen dollars; and butter, twenty-eight cents a pound. Farm laborers and men who hire out get two dollars and a half a week and board themselves.

Wherever we have been in Ireland we were delighted with the gay, bright flowers, almost, if not quite, equal to the flora of California. Some of the little mud cottages with thatched roofs were covered with daisies, white and yellow, and looked cheerful enough; and all along the road there was a great variety of flowering plants, among which the fox-glove (called the "fairy-slipper") was the most conspicuous.

We rode around Cork, a city founded by the Danes A. D. 1000. Several of the churches are worthy of attention—the Cathedral, St. Patrick's, St. Ann's, and the very ancient church of Shandon, with its thirty sweet bells, which I listened to until midnight, being kept awake by the characteristic volubility of the people around me. These bells are referred to by Father Prout in his

> "Bells of Shandon
> That sound so grand on
> The pleasant waters
>   Of the River Lee."

Our ride by car (stage-coach), about one hundred miles, to the Lakes of Killarney, via Glengariff, was full of intense interest. On the way we noted the ruins of many fine old stone castles, at least twenty-five in number, now almost hidden among the green of clambering vines. We enjoyed to the full this opportunity, while passing through the country, of seeing the Irish farms, their mode of cultivation, and the manner in which the people live. All along the valley, wherever there is a piece of ground large enough to insert a spade, they plant potatoes and corn, by which latter term they mean oats and barley, for with them all grains are "corn." I asked the driver, "Do you plant any corn here?"—meaning maize.

"O yes," he answered, "don't you see it?" pointing at the same time to the oats and barley.

The cabins are small, low, stone buildings, with thatched roofs, the doors just high enough to admit of entrance without stooping, and with one or two rooms six or eight feet by twelve, where the family lives with its chickens, ducks and pigs. The fire is of peat, which we saw donkeys carrying, a pannier full on each side, dug from the marshy ground; the floor is of earth, well swept, and clean and neat; no furniture is to be seen but a stool and a bed of boards, covered with straw and a few rags, in which all sleep together, or at least in pretty close proximity. In the corner, was piled, on a shelf against the wall, the delf, the clean, pretty plates of blue fronting us. It was disagreeable to notice that, almost without exception, the front yards contained a cess-pool, the ground being dug out so as to hold water, and then the accumulations alike from the household and the animals thrown in, to remain and greet continually the olfactories of the inmates. There are no windows, so they have a continual odor. You ask, "Why is this?" An intelligent Catholic priest who rode with us some distance, told us that they had tried to reform them in this; but long habit, the necessity of making compost for their land, the convenience of having a receptacle wherein can be thrown all refuse, and the fact that sites for cabins were selected hundreds of years ago, chiefly with reference to this said conveniency for land manure, altogether seemed to render it almost impossible to change their habits in this respect. The men, women and children look healthy and rosy-cheeked notwithstanding; but with us it would surely breed typhoid and other diseases. We asked the good Father, "Why not the same law of health here as with us at home?" He replied, "The cabins here have no windows; the people live largely out-of-doors, and, therefore, do not suffer so much from the effluvia."

Lord Bantry, who lives on Bantry Bay, by the side of which we rode for miles, owns an area of fifteen by forty miles of these lands, and rents them to these poor people. Rents, taxes and church-rates make their lives hard indeed. Nearly all the land of the country is owned by a few lords and rich proprietors, and these poor men own nothing. In fact, the land of Ireland is cultivated by six hundred thousand

VIEW OF THE LAKE OF KILLARNEY.
(Torc Mountain from Dinis Island.)

tenants, and owned by sixteen thousand landlords, of whom about two thousand possess two-thirds of the whole. It is not surprising, that, under such a system, there should exist Irish discontent.

Glengariff is a most picturesque place near the head of Bantry Bay, combining mountain and coast scenery in such perfection that Dr. H. thought it almost equal to the view in Lucerne, Switzerland. Here stands the old stone castle, now abandoned, dating from the time of the French wars; and Cromwell's Bridge, erected so that he could visit the O'Sullivan. From here over the Kerry Mountains, we wandered about Bantry and Kenmare Bays, the scene of many of the landings during the invasions of the French and others. The ride to-day was even more grand and picturesque than before. It culminated as we approached the Lakes of Killarney nearest to the mountains; while the last seven miles were along the three beautiful lakes called Lough Leane, Muckross and Upper, resembling somewhat Lake George, although not nearly so beautiful and picturesque. There is a legendary and poetic charm about them, as they are the scenes of all the O'Donoghue legends, from which have been formed so many stories and dramas; while Moore has immortalized one of the most charming portions of the lower lake in his "Sweet Innisfallen," and Lover (appropriate name) has clustered around them the most mischievous of memories, in his song,—

"Kate Kearney,
Who lives on the Banks of Killarney."

All about here is most delightful. Many of the estates and residences of lords and the old aristocracy were selected on account of the beauty of situation, with their lovely views of mountain and lake. Muckross Abbey is one of the finest mediæval ruins in Ireland. It was founded for the Franciscan friars, in A. D. 1100, by the McCarthys, Princes of Desmond. It is so luxuriantly umbrageous, that the ivy-covered building is not perceived until the visitor stands close beside it, and gazes upon the mouldering relics of antiquity.

The sepulchers of the ancient chiefs, among them those of O'Sullivan, Mor and O'Donoghue, are here, their tombstones still existing in different stages of decay, some with and some without epitaphs. The building consists of two principal parts, the church and the convent; the length of the former being one hundred and ten feet, its breadth twenty-four feet, while thirty-six feet is the length of the transept. It is divided into three compartments—choir, nave and south transept, at the intersection of which stands a square, massive tower of no great height. An elegant arched doorway, covered with a soft garb of ivy, forms the entrance, through which may be seen the great eastern window of the choir, in which part of the building the tombs are very numerous. The best preserved portion of the abbey is the cloister, in the center of which grows a magnificent yew tree, probably as old as the abbey itself, its circumference being thirteen feet. The refectory, the kitchen and the dormitories are still in good preservation, and the great fire-place that remains attests the attention that the friars paid to good cheer. The people tell you that Cromwell destroyed all these old castles and abbeys; they show you the hill from which he fired upon Blarney Castle, hitting the tower, whose injured portion is now upheld by iron rods. Irishmen, in truth, hate Cromwell, and if they wish to show their deep execration toward any one they cry, "The curse of Cromwell be upon you!"

II.

PARTING GLIMPSES OF THE EMERALD ISLE.... CATHEDRAL
RESTORATION..... WELSH SCENERY.... LLANBERIS....
SNOWDON.... CHESTER CATHEDRAL.... EATON HALL....
THE HOTELS.... RAILWAYS.

Llanberis, Wales.

ON Monday we came across the Irish Sea from Dublin to Holyhead, to make a tour through the "Switzerland of Wales," as it is called. We spent about ten days in Ireland, and were delighted with our visit, especially around the Lakes of Killarney, in favor of which much more might be said than can be written without kissing the "Blarney." The Sabbath was passed in Dublin, where we heard the Rev. Dr. Morley Punshon preach. He is one of the most eloquent Methodist clergymen in the world, and many of our friends remember the trouble he had with his denomination, in England, on account of marrying his deceased wife's sister. He came to this country, therefore, to gain a residence, and evade the law of England. The people here were delighted with his eloquent rhetorical periods and exquisite style, quite in contrast with his rather coarse, large *physique*. His sermon did not give me an impression of great sincerity, but rather seemed a rhetorical display of eloquent words. When he lectured in Columbus we were all pleased, and it appears to me that he is more popular on the lecture platform than as a profound and effective pulpit orator. Dublin is an old and substantial city, dating back to A. D. 140. The native Irish called it "Drom-Col-Coille" (the hill of hazel-wood). It is now four miles in length, and has nearly one thousand streets and many ancient and beautiful specimens of architecture, noticeable among which is Christ's Church Cathedral, erected A. D. 1038. It was here that the Church liturgy was first read in Ireland in the English language. The old Cathedral has just been restored, through the liberality of a Mr. Ray, a whiskey distiller, at a cost of £180,000 (about $900,000). Near this edifice, down Nicholas street, through the "Five

Points" of the city—a most wretched locality—stands the Cathedral of St. Patrick. Tradition points out this spot as the scene of very early religious rites in pagan times; but the earliest account of any Christian ceremony performed there is of the occasion when St. Patrick preached to the Irish during his efforts to convert them to the Christian faith. The sexton opened a well inside the Cathedral, and gave us a draught of water. The well, he said, was dug by St. Patrick himself, and thousands of bottles of the water had been taken to America. He informed us besides that the saint had dug the well to baptize the king and his newly-converted subjects, in A. D. 448. He showed us, also, the old stone font in the Cathedral where Cromwell watered his horses, and where he stabled them in the nave. The building was almost a ruin, a few years ago, until Mr. Guinness, the wealthy brewer, undertook to restore it—a work which has cost him £225,000 (about $1,125,000). In the interior are the monuments of Swift and Mrs. Esther Johnson, the "Stella" of his poems. There are also grotesque tombs of the Boyles, Schomberg, and others. If Mr. Ray and Mr. Guinness had underpinned and buttressed these old edifices, monuments of the past, and expended their money in building new cathedrals, their deeds might have been more worthy to embalm their memories in the coming years; for to me it seems a sacrilege to restore, as it is termed, these grand old architectural ruins. I begin to realize that we are moving among the stately monuments which still speak of the genius and wonderful creative skill of the past.

After visiting Bangor, Wales, and viewing the grand scenery from the top of the tubular bridge across the Menai Straits, which is eighteen hundred and fifty feet long, built by Sir George Stevenson at a cost of over three million dollars, we reached our present stopping-place, Llanberis, passing *en route* several thriving Welsh cities and Dolbadarn Castle, at Caernarvon, the birth place of Edward the Second, the first English Prince of Wales. It is a noble and picturesque ruin. At Llanberis we saw the beautiful lakes and waterfalls of the same name, embosomed among the Caernarvon Mountains, at the foot of Snowdon. We were advised to ascend the mountain during the night, in order to be ready to see the sun rise, from its summit, at half-past three in the morning, and accordingly procured our guide and ponies, and started up the mountain for an all-night ride, though the ascent to this highest elevation in Great Britain has obtained the evil repute that many persons in attempting it have perished on the way, and the attendant endeavored to interest us by relating the loss and destruction of some who had ventured up without heeding the advice of their guide. The fog and wind made the journey a cold and dismal one, and right glad were we, on reaching the top, to find a cabin with a comfortable fire. We waited patiently for the sun to rise. The time for his appearance came, but the fog was so thick that his majesty did not dispel it, and thus, like the " King of France," in the old song, " We marched up the mountain, and marched down again," without the view we had anticipated, although, in descending, we caught a glimpse of the grand scenery about us, and reached at length our good " homely" (home-like) " hotel," as the Welsh girl called it, who recommended us to go to the " Dolbadarn," established in 1708.

We took a top seat on the stage through " Llanberis Pass," passing the largest slate quarries in Wales, which employ three thousand men. In few places has nature been more grand in her handiwork than in this vale, which infinitely surpasses all works of art.

We stopped at Bettws-y-Coed. All the way the scenery has been most beautiful, where rivers, rocks, waterfalls and mountains present scenes of a diversified character. Taking the train for Chester, we passed through a beautiful country looking much like New England, though the houses are of stone, and many of them present a fine appearance. There were a great number of visitors among these Welsh mountains, which seem to be to England what the White Mountains are to our Eastern States at home. The weather has been so cold hitherto that we have been obliged to keep on our thickest winter clothing; but the thermometer has to-day mounted to 81 degrees, which is the warmest of the season. All through Wales we meet men who look like the Davis, Jones, Price, Hughes, Phillips and Williams families of Columbus, and we see their names as proprietors of hotels and other business establishments. The marked nationality, which betrays itself especially in language, is most strikingly apparent on passing the boundary separating either England, Ireland, Scotland or Wales.

Blossoms Hotel, Chester, England.

"Rare old Chester," wrote Albert Smith, in his "Struggles and Adventures of Christopher Tadpole." Chester is a walled city—the only one in Great Britain—two miles in circumference. "In A. D. 61 the walls were built by the Romans; in 73, Marius, King of the Britons, extended the walls; in 607 the Britons were defeated under the walls; in 907 the walls were rebuilt by a daughter of Alfred the Great; in 1224 an assessment for repairing the walls was made; in 1399 Henry of Lancaster mustered his troops under these walls; in 1645 the Parliamentary forces made a breach in these walls." As we go round these ancient walls one of the first objects of interest is Chester Cathedral, founded A. D. 1095. An attempt has been made to restore this old ruin, but it has been only partially successful through want of funds, for there are no rich brewers here who wish to perpetuate their names in Cathedral restorations. The verger, who showed us through the building, pointed out many objects of interest. The beautiful carving, which had been painted all colors of the rainbow, was now restored to its original oak, and is said to be the richest specimen of wood carving in Great Britain. Some of this beautiful work under the stalls for the monks was very ornate, among which, in their different stages, scenes of matrimonial quarrels were conspicuous. Canon Charles Kingsley once officiated here, and the present Dean is Dr. Howson, the eminent author, who, conjointly with Dr. Conybeare, wrote the Life of St. Paul, and other celebrated works of a kindred nature. A choral service was being held at the time, which we greatly enjoyed. The dean, two canons, vergers, organists, and ten boy singers were in attendance, and for an audience, there were some ten or fifteen women and ourselves. When they came in, the two vergers, with silver maces, marched in front, all presenting to one unaccustomed to it an attractive appearance. When the canon conducted any part of the service, the verger preceded him with the mace, and when he had finished that part of the service, would again precede him in like manner to the pulpit. It was refreshing to tarry awhile in this grand old Cathedral and worship God, surrounded, as we were, by so many vivid and solemn mementoes of the past. Here were the cloisters for the friars and monks of this once wonderful abbey, and their walks and places of meditation. The little, narrow oak seats around the walls, their places of rest in former times, exhibited, when raised, splendid carvings of historical events. Here were tombstones of quaint device and ancient date. All combined to make the hour an eventful one to us, and then the service was so beautiful and helpful! There are many things to interest us in this old Cathedral—monuments, rich memorial windows of stained glass, the gorgeous canopy of ancient oak adorning and supporting the fine organ, and that superb range of stalls, also of oak, four-and-twenty on either side, crowned with canopies of the richest tracery, and no one stall the copy of the other. As we stand and look around the magnificent nave, and note the taste and elegance which everywhere pervade it, we are struck with awe and admiration, and feel like exclaiming, "How all the resources of art have been brought to bear, by the creature man, in honor of his Creator, God!"

OLD PALACE, OR DERBY HOUSE, CHESTER.

As we start on our walk around the old wall of Chester, we come to an ancient tower rising above it, and upon it we read this inscription, "King Charles stood on this tower, September 24, 1645, and saw his army defeated on Rowton Moor." As we enter the tower an enthusiastic old man points out to us the battle-field and many places of interest about the city, and our minds go back, as we read over the quaint inscription that thus commemorates the fact that Charles the First stood on this very spot, and saw his gallant cavaliers borne down by the grim soldiers of Oliver Cromwell's army. At almost every step some object to recall the history of the past is brought before our notice—quaint old buildings of the sixteenth century, and other interesting objects, which we have not time to describe in a letter written as this is, "on the wing." One old house is pointed out to us, with the inscription, "God's Providence House," and it is said to be the only house in the city that escaped the plague in the seventeenth century. The owner carved upon the front: "1652. God's Providence is Mine Inheritance. 1652." They have curious names also for their hotels. Opposite "Blossoms," where we stopped, we can read the signs of the "Hop Pole Hotel," "Bear's Paw Hotel," and "Green Dragon Hotel."

It was in this quaint old city that Thomas Cole, who afterwards settled in America, and became celebrated as the painter of "The Voyage of Life," "The Expulsion," "The Course of Empire," and other noble works, was first put to school by his father, who then resided at Chorley, and it is interesting to recall the fact that while the rudiments of his education were received here, his first efforts with the brush were made in Ohio. There may still be persons living in Zanesville, Chilicothe or Steubenville who remember him.

We leave the city with regret; but we must have a row on the Dee. It was a beautiful day, and our boatman, an old citizen, who has followed his occupation on this classic stream for forty years, willingly pointed out to us all the objects of interest, and told us many things, on our way to Eaton Hall, about the Marquis of Westminster, the owner, who is the richest man in England. His income is said to be £1 10s. (about $7.25) a minute. This grand estate is thirty-six miles in circuit, whilst besides this he has other estates in Wales, Scotland, Berkshire and

London. The Marquis's son, the Duke of Westminster, resides on this estate, and while we were there he started for Manchester to attend a "Domestic Economy Congress" meeting. He is quite prominent in all moral and social reforms, especially in that of temperance. Both the Marquis and the Duke, his son, are liked by their tenants, and are popular with all classes. The estates are said to have belonged to the Chester Cathedral property when the Roman Catholics possessed it. No wonder that it has engendered bitterness in their hearts toward the Church of England to have all these grand old cathedrals and this immense church property taken from them. This was the first English estate we visited, and we found ourselves continually exclaiming, "What a pity that such vast estates could not be sold in small farms to the tenants, instead of having them entailed to sustain and perpetuate a great and powerful aristocracy!" In passing through one estate in Scotland to-day we traversed thirty-six miles. In fact, almost all the land in Great Britain is held in this way and cannot be sold.

Our ride up to Eaton Hall was a delightful one; our walk of seven miles through the grounds to Chester was on a broad, macadamized road, without a residence, except the lodge occupied by the gate-keeper and attached to the gates. This realized our dreams of an English park. A herd of from sixty to eighty red and spotted deer were seen feeding near the road, and rabbits and other wild animals started into flight at our approach. We visited the green-houses, and were told by the gardener that it took five miles of steam-pipe to heat them. Such rare shrubs and flowers, with their sweet perfumes, I never again expect to see.

Our journey from Chester to the English lakes has been through the large manufacturing and coal and iron districts. All speak of the manufacturing interests as greatly depressed; but there is not so much suffering among the operatives as in former years, as they have now learned to live more providently. I remember, some thirty years ago, to have heard Hon. Thomas Ewing, then United States Senator, deliver an address in Columbus on "The Downfall of England," founding his prophesy mainly upon a coal famine, which he supposed to be not far distant. On inquiry, I learn that such an event is not likely to occur for some centuries yet, and, judging from the price of coal, such a calamity need not be feared. The best anthracite coal is sold for from seven to nine shillings a ton, delivered in London, equivalent to $1.75 to $2.25 in our currency; and to the iron furnaces and rolling-mills is delivered at from four to six shillings, or $1 to $1.25 per ton; for the new discoveries made of late years have rendered coal cheaper than it was some years ago.

A well-informed manufacturer of London, whom we met on our travels, told us that American petroleum oil was sold for so much less than oil could be produced here that many of their large oil manufacturers were ruined, and, that if the supply continued, they would all be obliged to stop.

The newspapers this morning say that the experiment of bringing over live stock from America in sailing vessels proves a success. Five vessels arrived in this country last week with 1,825 head of cattle, and a number of horses and hogs. None died on the way, and only two had to be killed, and they were preserved in ice and brought to market here. This success is likely to have an important effect on English market prices for beef, and to increase the foreign demand in America. The weekly average arrival is from four to five thousand head. Prices are affected by the falling off in arrivals, and advanced one day on that account from seven and a-half to nine and a-half pence, or from fifteen to nineteen cents a pound. The best roasts and steaks bring from twenty-five to thirty-two cents a pound.

I had read for years that there was a much greater amount of intoxication in Great Britain than in the United States. In Ireland "mountain dew" (whiskey) was freely displayed at the hotels, and in England almost every one, men and women, drink ale and porter at their meals, and Scotch whiskey is recommended to us Americans to make us robust and healthy. Officers of churches are prominent dealers in "wine and spirits," and the clergy take a little for "the stomach's sake." Mr. O'Sullivant, Member of Parliament for Limerick County, Ireland, has introduced a bill providing that all spirits shall be detained in bond for at least twelve months before being permitted to be put on sale. It is not expected, however, that this will end the great evil of intemperance. At a recent investigation it was stated that an importer of whiskey admitted to an inspector that a moderate sized bottle of "French polish" would make a considerable quantity of wild whiskey. If "French polish," labeled "whiskey," is bonded for a dozen months, it comes out "French polish" still. We notice that the Catholic papers are earnest supporters of the temperance cause. We were informed that three of the Bishops and two of the Deans of Westminster Abbey were total abstainers.

Here, everywhere, women seem to have charge of the hotels, both in offices and bar-rooms. Men are seen sitting around little tables, drinking and smoking, while the women are attending to the office. The dining-rooms appear to be used as sitting and reading-rooms. The prices, so far, have been quite reasonable, averaging some $2.50 a day. It is always safe to make your bargains before you occupy your room; if not, there are likely to be a great many extras charged, for attendance, etc. Everybody wants a fee. They say, from Gladstone down to "Boots," make your bargains in advance, and you will be all right. You can travel in England, in third-class cars, at a penny a mile. Each car has four compartments, each compartment seating about six on each side, back to back. When the train starts, the doors are locked, and every one is fast until the next station, no matter whom they may have for companions. Should there be insane or drunken people, or even murderers among them, there is no remedy. The conductor, or guard, as he is here called, does not make his appearance until the next station. We have read of some startling experiences with the insane in these closely fastened cars, and that ladies have sometimes been insulted. An officer in the English army, of high social position, was lately tried and found guilty of disgraceful conduct to a young lady who was alone with him in one of these apartments. Trains make very fast time. One train, called the "Flying Scotchman," averages some sixty miles an hour between Glasgow and London, a distance of about four hundred miles.

III.

THE ENGLISH LAKES AND HOMES OF THE POETS.... AYR AND ROBERT BURNS.... GLASGOW: ITS WORKING PEOPLE, OPEN AIR SERVICES ON SUNDAY, THE OLD CATHEDRAL.... SHIP-YARDS ON THE CLYDE.... INVERNESS.... GLENCOE.... LOCH NESS.

Ayr, Scotland.

OUR visit to the English lakes was a most interesting one, not only on account of the beautiful scenery, but from the associations connected with them; so many of England's distinguished poets and authors having lived, written, and died there. Our first sail was by steam yacht around Lake Windermere. The residence of Prof. Wilson ("Christopher North") was the first place of note that met our view; then Mrs. Hemans's "Dove Nest," a little white cottage, was seen embowered amid the trees on the slope. After leaving the yacht, at the head of the lake, we take coach, and are enchanted with the lovely views of mountain and mere, and residences nestling by the waterside. The first house of special interest is "Nab Cottage," the humble white homestead on the roadside, by the margin of Rydal Lake, where Hartley Coleridge, the poet, lived and died. Next comes Rydal Mount, near the summit of which stands Wordsworth's house. The grounds are called Rydal Park, but no one is allowed entrance. The property is rented, and the occupant does not care to be annoyed by visitors.

We soon come to the quiet, smooth and beautiful Lake Grasmere; and then the first place to be sought is the church-yard, where Wordsworth's family lie buried, under a simple and modest slate-colored tomb-stone, about three feet in height, with the following inscriptions: "William Wordsworth, 1850;" "Mary Wordsworth, 1859." Beside them lies their daughter, and, next to her, her husband. Some other children of Wordsworth, who died young, are buried near. Close behind the family group is the monument of Hartley Coleridge, about two feet in height, of gray granite, and surmounted with a Greek cross and crown. Around the crown are the words,

HOME OF WORDSWORTH, RYDAL MOUNT.

"By Thy cross and passion, good Lord, deliver us," and under this comes: "Hartley Coleridge, born September 6, A. D. 1796, deceased January 6, 1849." The quaint old church near by, where they both worshiped, and the pews they occupied, were shown us, as well as a statue of Wordsworth in marble, in the church.

The vale of Grasmere is thus described by Wordsworth: "This vale of Grasmere, the loveliest spot that man hath ever found." On our return we took a path leading us by the house where Wordsworth first lived, and where he was visited by Sir Walter Scott and other authors. This path afforded us a splendid view of this whole region, of surpassing loveliness, and conducted us past Dr. Arnold's Fox Howe, and several beautiful homes under the mountains, with grounds laid out in English style, in lawns and flower-beds of almost every imaginable shape. I never walked over such velvety lawns, yet their effect and beauty seemed to me greatly injured by their being almost covered with such oddly-shaped flower-beds.

Our ride of twenty-two miles by coach in the morning was full of enjoyment, lying along the margins of Windermere, Rydal, and Grasmere, to Keswick, with thirty-four mountains in view, and in the vicinity sixteen lakes and eleven waterfalls. At Keswick we rode by the side of Derwent Water to the Cascade of Lodore, returning by row-boat. Near by is Greta Hall, where the poet Southey lived and died. In the graveyard adjoining the old Crossthwaite Church is his tomb-stone, in a recumbent position, with the following inscription: " Here lies the body of Robert Southey, LL. D., poet laureate. Born August 18, 1774; died March 21, 1843. For forty years a resident of this place. Also, of Edith, his wife; born May 20, 1774; died November 16, 1837. 'I am the Resurrection and the Life, saith the Lord.'"

We were allowed to enter Greta Hall, and were shown the poet's study, where he wrote more than one hundred volumes and one hundred and fifty articles—some of them, like that on Nelson, as big as a book—for different reviews.

We took the train, and were soon across the line into Scotland. On our way to Glasgow we made a detour to Ayr, the birth-place of Robert Burns. Before visiting his monument we called on his nieces,

Agnes and Isabella, aged respectively about sixty and seventy years. We were received most cordially. The elder sister asked to be excused, as she was engaged in washing dishes. She soon, however, came in. They live in a little, low, stone cottage, with thatched roof. Everything indicates a lack of this world's goods, yet all is neat and artistic, with flowers and pictures arranged about the room. They entertained us with talk about their uncle, and showed us a letter which has never yet been published; and, with true Scotch hospitality, offered us cake of their own making, from Australian flour, which they had had in the house for two years, and three kinds of wine—one being made by themselves from grapes grown in their own little yard. I could not resist the temptation to try the latter, but the Doctor steadily refused, as he always does, from principle.

We walked to the splendid monument erected to the memory of Burns, near the church and burial ground of his family, and also near the scenes of some of his beautiful poems. The Scotch are enthusiastic over Burns, and there were great crowds of excursionists from Glasgow, Paisley, and other cities, the day being Saturday, the afternoon of which is always a holiday for workmen. We thus had an opportunity of seeing the Scotch working people.

The working-men of Great Britain, from all accounts, seem terribly demoralized by drunkenness; and the skilled operatives are losing their genius and their power over other nations as superior workmen, by their dissolute habits, which seem to deaden their sensibilities. On the other hand, the manufacturers of the United States are fast taking the lead, and securing the markets of the world through means of their superior goods, which they produce at a price that enables them to compete with the English; and even American-manufactured articles of cutlery and silvered ware are sold in Sheffield. Some of the intelligent men that we met admitted this, and, when asked the reason, answered us, that "the working-men take Saturday as a holiday, and invariably get drunk, and on Sunday are unfit to go to church, and take Monday as their religious day; so that Monday is called 'Saint Monday,' as they lose so much time, and drunkenness unfits them for proper application to their duties."

There is great distress in Great Britain among working people. There are more persons suffering from hunger and want than at any previous time. The work-houses and poor-houses are overflowing. Many families are not able to buy meat, and live on bread and *beer*. The mills are not running, and the poor can find nothing to do, and despair seems to stare them in the face. The country appears overcrowded. Let them come to the United States, where there is room for them all, with our sixty times more land than England, though her population is nearly equal to our own. Whiskey and beer drinking are a terrible curse, and twelve times as much is spent for alcoholic stimulants as for clothing, which is enough to ruin any country. England's army also costs her more than we pay for all our schools. The laboring classes are not able to purchase a home, because the land is owned by a small number of large land-holders. More than half the land of Great Britain is owned by two thousand persons. These aristocratic gentry think less of the poor than of their thousands of acres for deer parks, and of having penal laws made, as if the very existence of the country depended upon "hares and rabbits." The Chatsworth estate, the seat of the Duke of Devonshire, through which we passed, contains two thousand acres for his private park, and thousands for farming. His flower-garden has two hundred acres. There are two thousand deer on the place.

We traveled for miles without seeing any house except two or three large castles, occupied by families living in great splendor; while at the villages may be seen the renters of the land, who are miserably poor, and hardly able to make both ends meet after paying their rents, taxes and church dues; "the abject slaves of the soil, whose sole hope in life is too often the work-house (that famous device against revolution, paid for by the middle class) and the pauper's grave." In talking with some of these renters, they say that "there is no inducement to try to any more than live; we cannot own a home; the laws are all made to protect the few thousand aristocrats, and thirty-two million souls are in their hands. The land-owner overrides all justice, takes precedence of all ordinary creditors on the helpless tenants of his estate, and controls the system of cultivation, often in utter disregard of private rights or private judgment; and, in addition, secures to himself the absolute reversion of every improvement which the tenant may make on the land." We asked one renter what rent he paid, and he replied, two thousand dollars a year for one hundred and sixty acres of land. He could buy four hundred acres of as good land as the sun ever shone upon, in Kansas or Nebraska, for what he pays for the rent of one hundred and sixty acres for one year. People are likely to waste money when they do not save it to buy homes. Small farmers are a conservative influence in our land. They pay taxes, and are deeply interested in an economical management of the affairs of the government. We said this to one of the large landowners, and he replied: "Our renters are satisfied; they set apart so much for taxes, so much for the church, so much for rent, and then live according to what remains from their income." In Ireland the poor people are not allowed to own a gun; they cannot fish in the lakes and streams, or hunt without a license; and if deer, rabbits or foxes come from the parks and destroy their crops, they have no remedy, and cannot shoot them.

Glasgow, Scotland.

Glasgow has a population of over half a million, and is the second or third city in Great Britain. We were impressed with the substantial appearance of the town. All the buildings are of stone, and its public edifices and churches are large and in a good style of architecture. Here we spent the Sabbath, and were struck with the crowds of well-dressed people on the streets, hurrying to and from church. Not a street car or public conveyance is to be seen, and only a few private carriages. No "wine and liquor" or drinking saloons are open, and all is quiet and orderly. As we pass through the thoroughfares to visit the cathedral, we notice at every corner, or prominent place, and park, orderly crowds, who seem quite attentive to lay preaching. A gentleman informed us that we should find out-of-door services in every part of the city from seven to nine o'clock, on Sunday nights, during the summer months.

The old Cathedral was founded A. D. 1133, though there was a church on the site as early as 539, and dedicated to St. Mungo or Kentigerne, the titular saint and founder of Glasgow. It is one of the few cathedrals saved from the mad fury of the populace, who sought to destroy, in these magnificent buildings, "the rookeries," as they styled them, lest the Popish prelates, "the rooks," should gather again. It was only saved by a prominent citizen threatening to shoot the first person that dared to touch a stone of the venerable pile. This cathedral has lately been "restored," and is unsurpassed by any other in Britain. The stained glass windows, which are considered fine works of art, add greatly to the beauty of the edifice. It is now owned or controlled by the Presbyterians, and whilst we were there services were being held. It seemed odd to witness the simple yet beautiful ceremonies of the Presbyterian Church conducted in so stately an edifice, and, as there was neither organ nor procession, it presented a striking contrast to the service we had so recently witnessed in Chester Cathedral. Leaving Glasgow, we made a tour through the Highlands, by the Scotch Lakes and Caledonia Canal, by which route we were informed that we should meet with the most picturesque and beautiful scenery anywhere to be found in Great Britain. Embarking on the new steamer Columba, on this her first trip, we noticed that the dock, for a mile at least, was lined with men, indicating that many people are out of employment. We learn that there is a strike among the men at work in the railroad shops, and hear also of serious strikes among all classes. Sailing down the Clyde, the great steamship docks and Atlantic steamers are in view. Upon this river are situated the most extensive yards for the building of iron ships in the world. Our new steamer is a magnificent one, costing two hundred thousand dollars. It is claimed to be the most perfect ideal of a steamboat as yet constructed, but they evidently have never seen our North River steamers. Her length is three hundred and eighteen feet, breadth of beam twenty-seven feet six inches. She is made entirely of steel, with steel boilers, and is the fastest sailer in Great Britain. Crowds line the docks at every stopping-place to look at her.

During our trip through the Scottish lochs, we passed many beautiful watering-places, and obtained fine views of the Dunglass Castle, with the monument arising amid its ruins, erected to the memory of Bell (who succeeded in launching upon the

Clyde, for practical purposes, the first steamer in the world, the "Comet"), and Dumbarton Castle, the residence of the Duke of Argyll. It is truly a lovely tour, winding around through the lakes, and our steamer accomplished twenty miles an hour. At length we arrived at Ardrishaig, and took a steamer going by way of the canal to Crinan, situated on Loch Crinan.

Inverness, Scotland.

Our ride for two days through the Caledonia Canal and various lochs (lakes), from Oban to this place, which is its northern terminus on Moray Firth, has been worthy to be long remembered. The valley through which the canal runs is sixty-three miles long. The proposition to construct the canal was first made after the suppression of the rebellion in 1745; but it was not until the beginning of the present century that the scheme was revived. The work did not meet the expectations of its projectors, although it cost five million dollars. In 1846 it was improved, at a cost of one million dollars. Although it has never been profitable, yet it is of great importance to the Highlands, and tourists certainly ought to feel grateful, as by this means they are enabled to view from the deck of a steamer some of the most sublime and picturesque scenery of the country.

We stop on the way at Ballachulish, and take coach for nine miles, through Glencoe, obtaining many views of surpassing grandeur, and tarry for the night at Corpach. While taking a walk to view some old ruins, we were accompanied by Dr. Donald Macleod, a popular preacher of Glasgow, editor of *Good Words*, and Chaplain to the Queen. He was stopping with Rev. Dr. Clerk, the Presbyterian minister of the parish, through whose kindness we were permitted to pass a delightful evening at the "Manse," and enjoy conversation and music in a refined and highly cultivated Highland home. Dr. Clerk is brother-in-law to Dr. Macleod, and the latter informed us that he was one of the most learned men in Scotland, and yet, for many years, had been settled over the very small congregation at Corpach, belonging to the "Old Kirk," and received his salary from the government; which gave him opportunity for leisure and study.

His wife and daughters were beautiful and intelligent, and quite inclined to compliment America and Americans, and American lakes and scenery. They seemed quite familiar with our authors, and the youngest daughter told me that she had just been reading "Uncle Tom's Cabin." Dr. Clerk asked his daughters to sing and play on the piano for us. They responded with some old Scotch ballads, joining with Dr. Macleod, who has a splendid voice. The music was restful and cheering, and artistically rendered. Dr. Clerk told us an anecdote of an old lady visiting Corpach, which lies at the foot of Ben Nevis, the highest mountain in Britain, its top being continually covered with snow. Seeing the snow on the mountains, she wondered if the women up there "kept their clothes out to dry all the time." In the morning we continue our journey by another steamer on the canal, and reach this place through forty-one miles of lakes and twenty-one miles of cuttings. This canal, intersecting Scotland from sea to sea, was planned to supersede the dangerous navigation of the Pentland Firth. Various old castles and ruins are pointed out to us, and almost every mountain and tarn has its own history, massacre or battle, connected with the various contending clans and parties in the past.

The longest loch through which we passed is Loch Ness, twenty-four miles long, and averaging one mile and a quarter in breadth, and its banks are clothed with birch woods to the water's edge. We stop and walk up the mountain about a mile to the Cataract of Foyers, a beautiful fall; but, as the streams at this time were not full, it disappointed our expectations. On our steamer there was a delightful company, mostly families traveling for pleasure, and an intelligent gentleman, noticing that we were Americans, and taking notes on our way, remarked that he had observed in a Glasgow morning paper that a telegram from the New York Herald Weather Bureau predicted rain in the north of Scotland on the fourth of July, and the prediction was confirmed by the rain driving us from the deck. He related a conversation with an old farmer, who had been greatly annoyed by the rainy weather in getting in his spring crops, and who had the old English prejudice against Americans. He said that when God Almighty managed the weather it was tolerably good, but since those Americans had got control of it it was outrageous, and he hoped the Almighty would resume his care of it soon, or the Americans would ruin their crops.

Inverness is of great antiquity. Cromwell's fort and other places of interest are to be seen from the top of Castle Hill.

I am writing now, at one o'clock A. M., without artificial light. It does not get dark, but only " a little hazy," as they call it, between twelve and one o'clock; and it is light enough to read out of doors, except during the hour above mentioned.

To-day is *our* " Independence Day," and it has been so cold that we were obliged to wear our winter garments and overcoats in order to keep comfortable. It is "fast day" here, which is observed twice a year in each parish by the Presbyterians, on the Sabbath previous to Communion. All business is suspended, therefore, in this district or parish, for it is their " Easter" day.

IV.

VISIT TO THE HEBRIDES.... THE TRADITION OF "LADY ROCK".... CASTLE OF THE "LORD OF THE ISLES".... FINGAL'S CAVE.... IONA AND SAINT COLUMBA.... REFLECTIONS.

Staffa and Iona Islands, Scotland.

WE spent a most intensely interesting day in visiting the islands of Staffa and Iona, two of the inner Hebrides, fifty-five miles from Oban, whence we take the steamer and sail up the Sound of Mull, skirting the most striking coast scenery which the Hebrides afford. The weather was most delightful, and the natural and picturesque scenery of the coast afforded us keen enjoyment, which was heightened by association with the historical events and traditions connected with the islands. In stormy weather the Sound is exceedingly rough, and its passage disagreeable. After leaving Oban, the famous "Dog-Stone" is pointed out to us, to which, according to tradition, Fingal was wont to tie his dog Bran, on his visits to Lorn. Lismore Light-House is seen on the western point of the island of Lismore—the "great garden," and before the Reformation the seats of the Bishops of Argyll and of the Isles. In passing the light-house, the "Lady Rock" is seen. According to tradition, "'Lady Rock' was the scene of a tragic episode in feudal times, which Campbell, the poet, has immortalized in his poem of 'Glenara,' and which forms the ground-work of the 'Family Legend,' by Joanna Baillie. The story is to the effect that Lauchlan Cathanach Maclean, of Duart, had married a daughter of Archibald, Earl of Islay, a progenitor of the Argyll family; but wishing to get rid of her, he conveyed her from Duart Castle to the 'Lady Rock'—one mile—and left her on it at low water, in the hope that she would be drowned when the tide rose. In this he was disappointed, for the cries of the lady brought some fishermen to her rescue, and when she got safe to land she made at once for her father's castle, at Inverary. Maclean shortly after went to Inverary, in deep mourning, to tell her father that his wife had mysteriously disappeared, but he was rather astonished to find her there before him, alive and well. On leaving the castle, Maclean was set on by a brother of the lady he had used so ill, and killed; or, according to another account, he was assassinated in Edinburgh."

The Sound of Mull is entered by a channel between the Grey Islands. We soon see the lofty basalt cliffs of Artornish, over whose wall-like front a torrent of great height falls after heavy rains, though the water never reaches the bottom in a body, being caught up by the wind and converted into spray. The ruins of Artornish Castle stand on a point of the same name, one hundred and three feet in height. "In this castle, in 1461, John, Earl of Ross and Lord of the Isles, held a parliament of his vassal chiefs, and dictated, as an independent prince, a commission to his beloved cousins, Ronald, of the Isles, and Duncan, Archdean of the Isles, to treat with Edward IV. and James, Earl of Douglas, for the conquest of Scotland. This was the last parliament held by the Lord of the Isles, as in a few years after the title became extinct, and the power of island kings passed away forever." We passed through a small lake, two and a half miles long, called Loch Alline, or "loch of the sun," at the end of which is seen the ruins of an old castle, said to have been built by a female chieftain of the clan Macinres, who, according to tradition, paid for it in an equal amount of butter. The entire trip, both going to and returning from Staffa and Iona, was full of intense interest, with picturesque scenery, the ruins of many old castles, and the passage of various lakes. Campbell, the poet, spent some time as tutor in one of these romantic places—a grand locality for a poet to garner imagery. Dr. Johnson also spent considerable time in this vicinity. The ruins of the house where he was entertained by Sir Allan Maclean, on a small island, can yet be seen. "He declared a Sunday on Inch Kenneth was the most delightful Sunday he ever spent in his life," and from this island he visited Iona in 1773.

We reached Staffa, which is about a mile in circumference and one hundred and twenty-nine feet high. Our steamer stopped long enough for us to climb the basalt rock, whence we get a view of Iona and various other islands, and the coasts of Mull. The basalt columns are regular and lofty. The same characteristics in the basalt of Staffa have been traced as in that of the Giant's Causeway. The great attraction here is Fingal's Cave, which is a marvelous sight; two hundred and twenty-seven feet long, forty-two broad and sixty-six in height, and having at ebb-tide twenty-five feet of water. It was a quiet, beautiful day, and, as our boatman rowed us into the cave, the walls pillared with basalt, in striking forms and grotesqueness of outline, and with effects of color tempered by the twilight of the cavern, reflected exquisite shadows in the waves. On this still, summer day the cavern, doubled in the sea, was a wondrous sight. The innermost vault of Fingal's Cave is reached by a slippery path along the tops of the broken columns, with a rope attached by holdfasts to the rock for support. All around Staffa the size and disposition of the pillars change. At one place, it is said, they are loftier than those of the Giant's Causeway. Some were disappointed at this splendid view, and, as one said, a contemplative mind is needed to enjoy it to its fullest extent. A solitary shepherd and his family at one time lived all the year round at Staffa; but he entreated to be removed, since in the winter gales the hollow roar made by the sea through these island caverns, sounded so dismally that he could not endure it. Bishop Van Troil has been humble enough to admit that Fingal's Cavern surpasses the architectural ruins

IONA CATHEDRAL.

of the ancients. Wordsworth writes, on hearing the fury which breaks against the pillared capes of Staffa:

> "Down-bearing with his whole Atlantic weight
>   Of tide and tempest on the Structure's base,
> And flashing upwards to the topmost height,
>   Ocean has proved its strength, and of its grace
> In calms is conscious, finding for his freight
>   Of softest music some responsive place."

Our sail to-day culminated on arrival at Iona, eight miles from Staffa. The island is three miles long by one and a half broad, and contains about two thousand acres of land, only six hundred of which are capable of cultivation. I cannot better describe the wonderful events which began on this island in A. D. 563 than by using the interesting account found in a little book published by Mr. James W. Miller, of Oban: "The rocky islet of Iona has filled a marvelous place in the history of Christendom. Chosen by some curious instinct as a refuge from outward dominion, on this isle the Christian faith survived a chaos which swallowed up the civilization of Rome. It needs some effort to believe that in this desolate place, in its most ancient form, was preserved and purified the Christian creed, when all continental lands were overrun with turbulence, and everywhere else was practiced the most dismal superstition. Like the sunset on the neighboring capes, the light of the world lingered in this sanctuary, and saints and apostles carried from its precincts the precepts and practices of Christianity to all other countries. Thirteen hundred years ago, Columba, with his twelve evangels, landed on the beach, and for nigh one thousand years the light they kindled remained uneclipsed. The pious, the learned, warriors, princes, the poor and the stricken—all turned toward Iona for counsel, for absolution, for a refuge, for alms. Christians sought Iona as they afterward journeyed to Rome and to Jerusalem; its shores were crowded with pilgrims, the sick and the maimed, beseeching a cure or a blessing. And not only was Iona the single island so blessed—Columba established thirty-two churches in the Western Isles, besides twenty-one which were scattered along the coasts of the mainland. To those were in time numbered the innumerable chapels or cells, relics of which are found on almost every isle of the Hebrides. In these dwelt solitary monks, away from all temporal allurements, and the benefaction of the pious. Isolated by the sea, they confirmed, by their own lives, the faith of their converts. Eschewing comforts and inured to poverty, these monks, amid their penances, were slaughtered by Norse pirates, and had their holy places given to the flames. No legends of Christian life are more pathetic, none have been so soon or so cruelly forgotten."

Columba was forty-two years old when he left Ireland, from which he was compelled to flee because of the bloodshed which arose on account of copying without leave the Psalter of his master, Finian. His purity has been recorded in the saying, "that he never told a lie nor looked upon a woman." The monks who accompanied him adhered to celibacy and no woman was allowed to land on Iona. Such was the superstitious reverence attached to Columba's life that it is believed that his old horse knew of his master's approaching death, from the fact of its laying its head upon his shoulder while he rested near Maclean Cross. He copied with his own hand, during his leisure hours, three hundred volumes of religious works. When death overtook him, on the evening of the 27th of June, A. D. 596, he had just reached the ninth verse of the Thirty-fourth Psalm.

Iona became the burial-place of kings and nobles. Forty Scottish kings, one king of France, two Irish kings, and two of Norway are among those buried here. Druidical relics were pointed out to us ; the old cathedral, in ruins ; the different monuments, with crosses and gravestones, the proportion of whose figures and the forms of whose decoration indicate a superior taste and knowledge of art. One needs days to examine the large number of monumental antiquities, and the mind can hardly grasp the fact that we stand on such sacred ground. For hundreds of years after the landing of Saint Columba, Iona was exposed to the attacks of heathen Danes, who, in A. D. 796, set fire to the monastery.

Iona has always attracted illustrious visitors, and Dr. Johnson wrote in regard to it: "That man is little to be envied whose patriotism would not gain force upon the plains of Marathon or whose piety would not grow warmer among the ruins of Iona."

We returned to Oban by the southern coast of Mull, and Kerrera Sound. Some Presbyterian clergymen came on board the vessel at one of our stopping places, who were pastors in the Free Church of Scotland, and their criticism of the Old Kirk ministers was severe in the extreme; insinuating that they were as fond as any one else of taking a little, if not sometimes a good deal, of wine for the stomach's sake. The Old Kirk is the State Church of Scotland, and receives its support from the government. The Free Church separated from it, and often there is one church of each denomination in small places, and sometimes the former has scarcely any members, although the good clergyman still continues to hold on to the "living." The Free Church ministers of Scotland seem proud of their success, and now number about as many churches and members as the State Church, from which they separated in 1843, on account of the State claiming jurisdiction over her spiritual affairs. It required great sacrifice of place, and even of their bread, for them to take the position they did—resign their livings, give up their churches and masses, on account of certain proceedings of the government affecting their rights and privileges. Dr. Chalmers and most of the great leaders of the Presbyterian Church of Scotland seceded. The pastors of the small, poor churches suffered most; and these men's description of what they endured, for conscience' sake—leaving their homes and going forth houseless—showed that they were men of no ordinary ability. More than 400 ministers went out to start new churches without government domination; losing their livings which they had received from the establishment. Such sacrifice and pluck makes one proud of Scotland and of the Presbyterian ministers; and no wonder the Free Church is taking the lead and is the most prosperous and aggressive! We can hardly realize how much we have learned and enjoyed, and feel like exclaiming that this has truly been a "red-letter day" in our calendar.

V.

THE TROSSACHS .... PERTH .... EDINBURGH .... MELROSE ABBEY .... YORK AND ITS CATHEDRAL .... CAMBRIDGE AND ITS UNIVERSITY.... NOTES AND INCIDENTS.

London, England.

OUR ride from Inverness to Edinburgh, a distance of about two hundred miles, was through the Trossachs, the last one hundred miles being through a country abounding in beautiful scenery and the theatre of stirring historical events. We passed through Grant-town, founded by Sir James Grant. Scotchmen claim that Gen. Grant's ancestors were from Scotland. When here, he visited the nieces of Robert Burns, at Ayr, and one of them said to him, " You are of Scotch descent, Gen. Grant?" He replied, " If so, it is so far back that I can hardly claim it; I am an American." She showed him one of Burns' letters to his brother William, pressing upon him to study "taciturnity," and she remarked to me that she thought Gen. Grant did not need any such advice, for he said scarcely anything during his visit. She thought that he was the most distinguished American living, and prized his photograph, which she showed to his wife; and Mrs. Grant promised to send her a better one when she returned to the United States, as the one she had was not a very good likeness. One of these ladies remarked that they had received a visit from ex-President Fillmore when he was in Scotland, and she considered him the finest looking man she had ever seen.

We passed through Blair Athol and Dunkeld. At the former place is the noble old castle of Blair, the ancient residence of the dukes of that name. It is traced back to the thirteenth century. The district around is the best hunting ground in Scotland, and is the scene of many historical events. From Dunkeld Station we obtain a view of Dunkeld Cathedral. The place is beautifully situated among wooded hills, on the northern bank of the Tay, and is of great antiquity, claiming to have been the ecclesiastical capital of Scotland during the ninth and tenth centuries. Sir

Walter Scott wrote several songs suggested by historic events in this district.

We afterwards visited Perth. Among the many incidents of history related of this place is one stating that "In 1545-6 five men and a woman were burned here for heresy; and it may also be said that the Reformation in Scotland began in Perth, as John Knox preached here some days after his return to the country."

Edinburgh did not disappoint us. It is certainly one of the most beautiful cities for natural situation that we ever saw. Standing upon three hills, from every point the city appears to great advantage. It is divided into the old and new towns. We have a splendid view from the old Castle, with the sea in the distance. The first places visited were the Palace and ruined Abbey of Holyrood, the former founded by James V. and the latter by King David I., in 1128. The most interesting part of the history of this palace —a history of stirring events and well-known personages—was the fact of its being the residence of Mary Queen of Scots, with whose eventful life almost every reader is familiar. We are shown the picture gallery, one hundred and fifty feet long by twenty-seven broad, decorated with pictures of one hundred and six Scottish sovereigns, "who lived from the time of Fergus, before the Christian era, to James VII." Many interesting relics of Queen Mary are pointed out, among them the private stair by which Rizzio's assassins ascended to Mary's apartments, and the stain of the blood, said to be Rizzio's, at the entrance to the audience chamber. It requires some faith to believe it, as well as many other things related in all seriousness. The old palace is a splendid specimen of architecture. Queen Mary's portraits, seen in both palace and castle, show that she was indeed a beautiful woman. The room in which James VI. was born, is not more than eight feet square, with a recess of about three feet at the window. Then there is the crown-room, containing the ancient regalia of Scotland—crown, sceptre, sword of state, etc. The crown jewels are valued at one million dollars.

The view of the city from the old Castle walls one wishes to enjoy for hours. Another view is from Arthur's Seat, a mountain rock about eight hundred feet high, which seems as if it were in the city, though covered with grass and used as a sheep pasture. The view is a grand one, commanding as it does both city and surrounding country.

On our way to London we visited the ruins of Melrose Abbey, about thirty-six miles from Edinburgh —larger and more perfect than anything of the kind we have yet seen. The finest feature is the great eastern window, thirty-seven feet high and sixteen broad. We also visited Abbotsford, erected by Sir Walter Scott, at a cost of two hundred and fifty thousand dollars. His library consisted of twenty thousand volumes, and the dimensions of the room are sixty by fifty feet. The drawing-room is richly furnished. The walls of the armory are covered with old muskets and many other ancient instruments of war, coats of mail, etc., arranged by himself. In another room are a copy of one of his writings, the jewelry and other articles presented to him, and in a glass case the clothes worn by him just before his death. The situation of the house is low, and one cannot see why such a location was selected, since the country about abounds in hills and beautiful building spots.

We came to old York, England, to spend the Sabbath and worship in the cathedral, regarded as the most splendid in Great Britain, whose length is five hundred and twenty-four feet, and whose nave is one hundred feet in height. Our State House in Columbus is, I think, about three hundred feet in length, so that one can easily estimate the relative proportions of the buildings. This old Cathedral, York Minster, is in the form of a cross, and is considered one of the finest in the world. It was begun in the seventh century, but was principally built in the thirteenth and fourteenth. We heard a first-rate total abstinence temperance sermon from Rev. Canon Wilberforce, a grandson of the late Hon. William Wilberforce, England's great reformer and anti-slavery agitator. The sermon had the true ring to it, but was evidently not enjoyed by the worshipers, as we see everywhere, at hotel tables, that nearly all, men and women, drink either ale or porter. We noticed printed cards in the seats as follows: "Memorial Church to the late Bishop Wilberforce. Rector, Rev. Canon Wilberforce. Canon Wilberforce is extremely anxious to add one bay of the nave, to be built exclusively from the contributions of temperance well-wishers, to be surmounted by a brass plate, inscribed to this effect. The cost will be £1,000, some £200 of which has already been subscribed by various temperance societies. He earnestly solicits the aid of his brethren in the teetotal cause," etc. We went in the afternoon to the choral service, and if we had not known that we were in a Protestant cathedral, we should have supposed we were where the full Roman Catholic liturgy was used in all its ceremony and display.

The city of York, from which New York derived its name, is the capital of Yorkshire, situated about midway between Edinburgh and London, some two hundred miles on either side. It was the scene of most important events during the successive struggles of the Britons, Saxons and Danes. Constantine the Great is said to have been born here, A. D. 272. "In A. D. 521 King Arthur kept Christmas in York, said to be the first celebration of that festival held in England."

The view across the great transept of the Cathedral is said to surpass, in architectural effect, that of any other Gothic edifice. The deanery, chapels and canons' residences give to everything a grandeur and lavishment of wealth and a religious display hardly realized by those who first enter the old country from America. I had heard and read of, and had longed to visit this famed cathedral pile, and judge for myself, and find I had received no adequate conception either from reading or pictorial illustration. The great east window in this cathedral is seventy-five feet high by thirty-two feet wide. It is one of the glories of the building, and is the largest window in the kingdom that retains its original glazing. The contract for glazing between the Dean and Chapter and John Thornton, of Coventry, is dated 1405. He was to receive for his own work four shillings a week, and finish the window in three years. There are two hundred compartments, each about a yard square. The subjects in the upper division, above the gallery, are from the Old Testament, beginning with the Creation and ending with the death of Absalom. All below are from the Book of Revelations, except those in the lowest tier, which are representations of kings and bishops.

On Monday, after our study of the grand old Cathedral, we felt it a pleasure to visit " Scrooby," where the first Congregational Church was organized. " The three simple points," says Professor Hoppin, of Yale College, in his book entitled " Old England," " upon which Elder Brewster and his co-religionists founded their right of separation from the Established

Church at that time were these: 1. The determination not to support and attend upon many prescribed ecclesiastical forms, not perhaps vested in themselves, but inwoven with ordinances and opinions that they esteemed Popish. 2. The claim to the right of individual interpretation of the Scriptures. 3. The assertion of the right to exclude immoral persons from their Church Communion. These points of difference compelled them to be separatists; not only driving them to a separation from the Church of England, but from their native soil, and finally compelled them to become 'strangers and pilgrims' on a totally new and foreign shore. The Pilgrims under Brewster were mostly unknown— Lincolnshire ditchers and plain Nottinghamshire farmers, with now and then a yeoman and a man of family and education. They were, however, sound, honest, thoughtful Englishmen. The Church thus established was organized in 1602, and was the model of all our 'Congregational' churches. They went first to Amsterdam, afterward returned to England in the *Speedwell*, and finally embarked in the *Mayflower* from Plymouth. These were the 'Pilgrim Fathers.' Such were the men who were gathered together in that small, despised, religious communion, and who came to the new world to plant, unconsciously, and, as a natural result of their religious views, the principles of a free republic." We find here only the lonely and decayed manor-house stables, in which Brewster preached, now occupied as a house. We were shown his pulpit, library (" a bit of a cupboard," as the old lady who showed us around expressed it), and a niche in the wall where he kept his wine; and in the buildings some carved wood-work and ornamental beams, covered with dust and cobwebs, which belonged to the Archiepiscopal Palace. There are only about two hundred inhabitants here, and a small church edifice, where Episcopal service is held once every Sabbath, the rector receiving £100 (or about five hundred dollars a year). The manor-house is in the midst of marshy surroundings, " and to think of what vast influences and activities have flowed from this quiet and almost listless scene, one has strange feelings." Do you wonder we enjoyed the contrast with York Cathedral?

Our ride from Scrooby to Cambridge gave us an idea of Old England's country scenery, seeming, as it were, through a city dotted with small farms like garden-spots; with their little patches of grass, wheat, barley, oats (no maize anywhere to be seen), garden vegetables and lavender. Very few handsome farm-houses are to be seen, such as can be met with on most of the roads leading from Columbus. The large towns and cities, as you approach them, look like new brick-kilns just opened; for the buildings are of brick, and the roofs of clay tile, making everything appear red and "bricky." The most beautiful and attractive places are the manses or rectories (or, as we should call them, parsonages), attached to the churches. We noticed this alike in Ireland, Scotland and England. The grounds about these buildings are spacious, laid out with taste, surrounded by hedges, and adorned with vines, plants and flower-beds. We thought it no wonder that these "livings," or rectorships, should be sought for and purchased by those desiring an opportunity to cultivate their taste, and study, and live a life of ease and pleasure.

We stopped at Peterborough to see another old cathedral, measuring four hundred and seventy-one feet in length by one hundred and eighty in breadth.

Here were buried Queen Catharine and Mary Queen of Scots—the latter now removed to Westminster Abbey. Peterborough Abbey was destroyed about 807, and restored in 966, A. D.

We passed Huntingdon, the birth-place of Cromwell. Cambridge, where we stopped over night, is celebrated for its great University. There are seventeen different colleges, with separate corporations and officers, holding the buildings and libraries and large funds in money, lands, etc. Trinity, King's, St. John's and several other colleges were visited, in whose libraries, among other treasures, we were shown the original manuscript of Milton's "Paradise Lost," and also the original of the "Old Covenant," signed in blood. The University library has half a million volumes—one of the earliest Bibles, written in the sixth century, also "The History of Troy," translated by Caxton and printed by him about the year 1475, and many ancient manuscripts. There are two thousand students in the colleges, the grounds of several of which extend across the River Cam, from which Cambridge received its name. The large old trees arching the walls, the lawns and flower-beds and river, give to all a delightful appearance, and one could easily dream away his time under the shady boughs by the banks of the stream, forgetful of high honors to be obtained by hard study. In one of the large courts of Trinity College, two hundred feet square, with a lovely fountain in the center, surrounded by flower-beds and a velvety lawn extending to the stone buildings, four stories in height, occupied by the students, we noticed at the base of each window a wooden box painted green, about a foot high and the width of the window, full of scarlet geraniums and other showy plants in full blossom. Here were hundreds of windows, from the first to the fourth story, around the inclosure, lighting up the old dingy stone buildings wonderfully. The rooms of the students were elegantly furnished. Each student has a sleeping-room and parlor. Their meals are ordered as in a hotel, and some of them, at eleven o'clock A. M., were just taking their breakfasts. Everything here appears to indicate that even a student in moderate circumstances could enjoy the advantages of these grand old institutions. One young man informed us that, with reasonable demands, the expense might be limited to from fifteen to eighteen hundred dollars a year.

So many colleges in one place cause great rivalries among the students. Trinity College boasts, among her graduates, of Bacon and Newton, whose portraits, in full length, together with a large number of other distinguished men, grace the apartment where so many have supplied the wants of the inner man. The old dining-hall looks like a chapel, with its large Gothic windows and high Gothic ceiling. Christ's College claims Milton as one of its graduates. They show you here his full-length portrait, and in the grounds the old mulberry-tree that he planted. These seventeen colleges, with their various buildings, are of stone, and situated in different parts of the city, although in one locality several are not far apart. These, with the University church, and various other old churches, give to the city an appearance of one great educational center, as certainly it is one of the greatest in the world.

We have now been through Ireland, Wales, Scotland and a part of England, running up through the last two on the east and returning on the west side to London. We could not have wished for more delightful weather, having been detained only one day by rain. We were advised to "marry to an umbrella" on our arrival, but as yet we have not done so. We have found hotels at moderate prices with but one exception—at the Maclean's Hotel, Glasgow. It is a splendid hotel—almost equal to the Windsor in New York. Our arrival was on Saturday. The guests were few, and no regular dinner was served. We ordered a plain dinner and a cup of tea, and when our bill was sent in, on Monday morning, dinner was charged at $1.12 each, and tea at fifty cents a cup, making the entire charge for the meal $1.62 each, with everything else in proportion. At the Waverley Dining-rooms, in Edinburgh, the charge for a better cup of tea was 2d. or four cents, while other things were equally reasonable. The less pretentious hotels were generally our choice. Sometimes they were even ancient looking, though within we found them neat, hospitable and clean, always with flowers adorning the apartments and with beautiful little yards laid out in beds of flowering plants, and sometimes the smaller hotels were covered with clambering roses, rivaling in size even Underwood's Chromotel and Marshal Neil, and in the greatest profusion. The hotel at which we are stopping here, "The Old Castle" ("The Bull" is the popular hotel), is antiquated enough. The building was erected in 1620, and is so quaint and odd that we begged a photograph of it. They supply us with the nicest French rolls we ever ate, and everything else is abundant and good; charges about two dollars a day. One can spend a "mint" of money if he chooses, and Americans are generally so lavish that the hotel people and everybody else consider them fit subjects for plunder. Some Germans who were traveling with us, and made no previous bargain for their entertainment at a different hotel from ours, showed us their bills, which were more than double our own. I do not think we have seen men as managers or conductors in the office or bar (they are both one) in any hotel. No men are about except "Boots" and the table-waiters, who are habited in black dress suits, white cravats, and with hair oiled and parted in the middle. You would think they were the *élite* of the place, just ready for a ball. Women receive you at the door cordially, and sometimes gracefully. Women show you to your rooms; women make out your bills, and women deal out the ale, porter, brown stout, whiskey, etc. There are said to be one hundred thousand beautiful girls in England employed in saloons, tending the bars. The handsomest and most graceful are selected, as an attraction to the young men; for, as we have said, the office and bar-room are one, and all classes resort thither to smoke and drink. At one place in London we saw from twenty to thirty girls in a large and brilliant restaurant, all dressed neatly in black, and at least one hundred young men smoking and drinking, while the girls served out to them their whiskey, brown stout, and other drinks. One young Englishman with whom we traveled, and who seemed anxious to criticise Americans, and to touch some tender spot, said: "You have the Mormons." "Yes," Dr. H. replied; "but they are mostly increased by immigration from Europe." The Englishman further said: "You have women's rights." "Yes," said Dr. H.; "but we should consider it indelicate to have our women deal out liquors and tend bar; the 'lady-waiter' saloons are closed, and both proprietors and waiters are marched off to jail." The Englishman subsided. Women run the hotels, and do it well, so that one would think that they were the proprietors themselves. Cannot they do anything they undertake?

VI.

FIRST VIEW OF LONDON......THE AMERICAN MINISTER ......WESTMINSTER ABBEY AND TOMBS OF THE POETS....HOUSES OF PARLIAMENT AND BUCKINGHAM PALACE... ENGLISH EQUIPAGES AND PUBLIC PARKS.

London.

OUR ride from Cambridge to London was through a flat, uninteresting country. We are now in this grand metropolis, the most interesting to Americans of all the great cities of the Old World, from the fact that it is the largest city of the civilized world, and contains a population of about four millions, and covers a space of about twelve miles by ten. After seeking a homelike resting-place with Mr. and Mrs. Burt, where friends in Columbus advised us to stop, we started out, with a letter to our United States Minister to the Court of Saint James, Hon. John Welsh, who

WESTMINSTER ABBEY.

received us cordially, inquiring after Columbus acquaintances, and offering to give us tickets of admission to Parliament and to the Queen's Stable at Buckingham Palace, and any other favor he could grant us. Our first visit was, of course, to Westminster Abbey, with its wonderful aisles, arches, and forests of noble columns. Historians have fixed the era of the first Abbey in the sixth century. The interior of the Abbey is three hundred and seventy-five feet long; breadth, two hundred feet; height, from pavement to inner roof, one hundred and one feet; and to sky-light, or lantern, as it is called, one hundred and forty feet. It is well we visited the other celebrated English Cathedrals first. Although York Minster is superior in architecture, this is more historic and interesting, with its nine chapels, containing tablets and reclining statues and the tombs of kings and queens from the tenth century. But to an American these are of little interest in comparison with the tombs and statues and inscriptions in the Poet's Corner—of Shakspeare, Chaucer, Campbell, Thomson, Wordsworth, Dickens, Bulwer, Charles Kingsley, and, indeed, many of the most prominent British writers and poets. The architecture of the

Chapel of Henry VII. is a feature of general admiration—the chapel containing the magnificent tomb of the founder, and those also of Queen Elizabeth and Mary Queen of Scots. The gold-mosaiced altar tomb of Edward the Confessor stands in the chapel of Saint Edward, together with the coronation chairs in which every sovereign of England since Edward I. has been crowned. Here, indeed, one may spend a day with great interest.

The Houses of Parliament are near Westminster Abbey, and help to add, by their two lofty towers and the elaborate finish of the immense stone structure, to the contrast and effect of the old walls and grand buttresses of the Cathedral. To vary the scene, we make a visit to Buckingham Palace, the London residence of the Queen—an immense, plain, stone building, which looks as low and flat as our Ohio Penitentiary, and not as attractive in architectural style. We should judge that it is as large as the latter building, and only occupied when the Queen visits London.

Everywhere we see the immense expense attendant upon keeping up royalty, and impressing upon the people its wonderful power and dignity. We

HOUSES OF PARLIAMENT.

visit Marlborough House, the residence of the Prince of Wales, and then St. James' Park and Kensington Gardens, large parks,—the former containing about ninety acres, with handsome drives and lawns, enriched with lofty trees. The lake is a famous skating place in the winter, and the park is a delightful resort for children and others. This is considered one of the greatest ornaments in the metropolis, and we had a fine opportunity to view the splendid English turn-outs, with their coaches and four, with various out-riders, dressed in all styles of livery, with rosettes on their hats, and white knee-breeches. The horses and carriages do not look so stylish as those you see in Central Park, New York, on a pleasant afternoon; and what greatly mars the looks of the horses is the cutting off of about half the tail of each, which gives them all such a bobby appearance. We have not seen a horse since we came into Great Britain but what had his tail thus mutilated. We asked several times, " Why do you cut off the horses' tails in this way?" The only answer is, " Because it makes them look tidy."

VII.

London Tower.... Kew Gardens.... The National Gallery.... A Royal Display and Garden Fête.... The Queen's Stables.... The London Slums.... The Pulpit Orators of London.... Curiosities at Kensington Museum.... Environs of London.... Royal Academy.... Bank of England.

London.

IT takes some days to realize that one is in a city of nearly a million more inhabitants than the whole State of Ohio contains. There is such a mass of people that the inclination arises to exclaim, "I am a mere bubble, a speck, on this immense sea of existence! I am worthless and insignificant in the eye of God." We walked the streets for miles, and mounted the tops of omnibuses, in order to see the prominent buildings, etc., of the city. If our High Street Omnibus Company would have their omnibuses arranged, as here, to carry as many or more on the top than on the inside, it would be a saving of the number of horses and drivers employed, and make an attractive, pleasant place on which to ride. We then wound our way to the "Tower." We had read about it in our youth, and wondered what such a place of torture and imprisonment looked like. Instead of one great tower, as we supposed, it consists of a cluster of houses, towers, barracks, armories, warehouses and prison-like edifices, situated on the Thames. It is the ancient fortress and gloomy state prison of London, and historically the most interesting spot in England. The Normans began the erection of the "Tower" in 1079. We saw twenty-two equestrian figures, in full equipment of armor, consisting of kings, queens and old warriors, which give one an idea of the ancient manner of protection against lance-thrust, arrow and bullet, and carry one back into the past. One cannot remember the long list of the distinguished and the notorious who, during the past eight centuries, have been beheaded and have perished within these walls. The implements of torture, the beheading block, and thousands of other ancient things pertaining to war and imprisonment, are seen—enough to give a man the nightmare for the balance of his life. There can be no sadder spot on earth. The crown jewels, which are preserved in a glass case, protected by a strong iron cage, were shown us. Among them is Queen Victoria's crown, adorned with two thousand seven hundred and eighty-three diamonds. All of the regalia in this glass case, about ten feet in diameter, is valued at from fifteen to twenty millions of dollars.

On another day we were glad to go some ten or twelve miles into the country and visit Kew Gardens. The flower-beds, hot-houses and conservatories are numerous, where ferns, orchids and cacti are particularly interesting. Immense sums have been laid out here by the Government, and the gardens are kept up by employing most celebrated botanists, who obtain rare plants from all parts of the world. The Palm House, reaching to a height of sixty feet, cost one hundred and fifty thousand dollars. The large Fern House contains one thousand different varieties of ferns, of which there are sixty varieties of adiantums. The gardens are seventy-five acres in extent, beautifully laid out in flower-beds, and present a gay and lovely appearance; while two hundred and forty acres are laid out in walks, with rows of trees, where one could spend days in admiration and enjoyment.

Our visit to the National Gallery was one long to be remembered. This gallery is one of the finest in the world. There are one hundred and ten paintings in oil by Turner, and even more landscape sketches in water colors by the same master (the latter sketches being loaned by Ruskin). I do not, as a general thing, like his paintings. They are too indistinct and shadowy and fairy-like; but who can help praising them when Ruskin considers him the greatest of English painters? One of the most beautiful, as the sun came out and shone suddenly upon it, was his "Bridge and Palace of Caligula,"—to which bridge (the work and caprice of the tyrant) old Suetonius has the following reference:

"Bajarum medium intervallum Puteolanas ad moles ponte conjunxit."

The picture, as we have said, is an exquisite one: on the left are seen the ruins of the palace, and on the extreme right, in the distance, the shores of Baiæ; children are sporting with goats in the foreground, while the sun is rising behind the ruins. Caligula, in order to confute a prophesy made by Thrasyllus, a mathematician, declaring that he would no more be Emperor than he could drive his chariot across the Bay of Baiæ, had constructed a bridge of boats from the mole at Puteoli across the bay, upward of three Roman miles, which he actually both rode and drove over. The Bridge of Caligula was necessarily temporary; but Turner has assumed in his picture a structure similar to that of the mole, extending completely across the bay, and has in his MS. poem, "The Fallacies of Hope," given the following description of it:

> "What now remains of all the mighty bridge
> Which made the Lucrine Lake an inner pool,
> Caligula! but massive fragments, left
> As monuments of doubt and ruined hopes
> Yet gleaming in the morning's ray, that tell
> How Baiæ's shore was loved in times gone by?"

The paintings in the grand gallery are among the finest in the world, comprising works by Raphael, Correggio, Rubens, Murillo, Rembrandt, Leonardo,

Titian, Wilson, Reynolds, West, and others, many of which are the originals of the fine engravings given in "Art Treasures of England," a recent publication, and one largely subscribed for in Columbus. Some of the paintings cost seventy thousand dollars. The funds to keep up the Gallery are provided by Parliament, about fifty thousand dollars a year being granted. One needs to spend a month here to fully enjoy and appreciate such a vast and rare collection.

One day, in passing up Pall Mall, near Marlborough House, we saw a great crowd gathering. Inquiring the cause, we were informed that there was to be an afternoon "garden party" at the Prince of Wales's residence, and that the Queen would be there, coming, as she always does, in great state from Windsor Castle. Of course, we stopped with the crowd. Great preparations seemed to be going on. First, about one hundred police, in full uniform, marched in through the Pall Mall gate; then a company of British red-coated soldiers; then a band of musicians, about one hundred in number; then came the Prince of Wales, preceding the Princess with their three children, looking as sweet and pretty as those of other people; then, for two or three hours, came the British aristocracy in splendid equipages; the foreign ministers; Gladstone; Baron Rothschild (an old, decrepit man), walking; the Duke of Connaught, the Queen's third son; the Earl of Granville; Duchess of Wellington; Earl and Countess of Dudley, the latter being very beautiful. These and many more were pointed out to us. Soon great excitement was everywhere manifest, and two knights on horseback came riding up the street at full speed, carrying a lance with a scarlet flag. Then a dozen gay outriders in half armor, looking like our Knights of Pythias; then came the grand state carriage, with four gray horses and various footmen, and everybody became aware that it was the Queen, with her daughters, the Princess Louise (wife of the Marquis of Lorne) and Princess Beatrice. A slight cheer went up as the Queen passed. She is a robust, red-faced, well-preserved woman of about sixty, looking not over forty or fifty, and has nine children, all living—five sons and four daughters. The sons seem to inherit their mother's avarice and love of power, and the daughters Prince Albert's generosity and mental capacity. For two or three hours, nearly as fast as they could enter the gate, came the splendid equipages,—mostly open carriages,—giving us a fine opportunity to see the ladies in full dress. Many of the young ladies were in white swiss or white silk and satin. Most of the older married ladies were in plain black silk. Only a few were on foot. One lady alone, with a footman behind, drove a pair of gray horses, in a Victoria phaeton.

We made a visit to the Queen's stables, at Buckingham Palace, in which are kept about one hundred horses, for the use of the royal establishment in London, and about the same number are kept at the Windsor Palace, all of the best blood that can be obtained, with gold and silver-mounted harness and carriages to match. The great State carriage of George III., which is used only on coronation occasions, looks like one of Barnum's grand parade band chariots. It is one hundred years old, weighs four tons, and cost over fifty thousand dollars. On the doors and sides are some original paintings, by Cipriani, which are valued highly. Some sixty men are employed as grooms about these stables in London. The Queen's own horses are nine cream-colored stallions, and are used only on State occasions. At Windsor Castle she keeps the same number of gray horses. All the horses in the stable but these have "bob tails."

Our landlord asked us to accompany him to a different scene from those we had witnessed during the day, and about nine o'clock at night we were divested of watches, money and jewelry, and started out to see the "slums" of London. Such squalor and poverty were heart-rending; but the saddest sight was at the drinking-places. There were more women drinking and drunk than men, and they were altogether the most boisterous and belligerent. We saw here so many to remind us of Dickens's characters, as portrayed in his books—characters so often selected from the poorer and lower classes. Every now and then we would come across a temperance saloon with bathing-rooms, or "coffee taverns," as they call them in England, showing that benevolent people are at work. The temperance advocates have formed large corporations, called "Coffee Tavern Companies," of prominent men of wealth and reputation, to operate these taverns in different parts of London. The one we visited, called the "Morton

Arms," has seven branches, called "The Glass House," "The Market Tavern," "The Temple Arms," "The Tom Hughes," "The Cross Keys," "The Phœnix Tavern," "The Red Boot Tavern,"—curious names to us. Other houses are in course of adaptation all through London. The design is to make these places attractive to working people, and they generally seek a place near some liquor-selling tavern where the working men congregate, and their intention is to make the temperance taverns more attractive than the others, and offer a "bill of fare" at lower prices. Here is the "price-list" and notices on the bill of fare:

Cocoa, per cup	1 d. = 2 c.
Coffee, "	1 d. = 2 c.
Tea, small cup, per cup	1 d. = 2 c.
Tea, large cup, "	2 d. = 4 c.
Small plate of beef	2 d. = 4 c.
Large " " "	4 d. = 8 c.
Small " " ham	2 d. = 4 c.
Large " " "	4 d. = 8 c.
Seed and currant cake, per slice	1 d. = 2 c.
Bread and butter	½ d. = 1 c.
New milk, per glass	1 d. = 2 c.
Boiled eggs, etc., etc., etc.	

The Company will also supply lemonade, gingerade, soda water and other aerated drinks, in bottles and by the glass, at 1 d. and 2 d.

Good cigars to be had at 2 d.

N. B. Non-alcoholic beverages, 1½ d. per bottle.

Working men may bring their own meals and eat them on the premises.

Everything good and clean.

Out-door trade done. Customers bringing their own jugs or cans will be supplied.

I have been particular in describing the above on account of the success attending these taverns in attracting the working men and their families, and as a financial investment. Gladstone, the Lord Chancellor, and the leading reformers are interesting themselves in this good work. Here is something practical for us at home to adopt, where intemperance is becoming a national disgrace. These coffee taverns, I am told, become self-supporting. Reading-rooms, smoking-rooms, and everything to entice young men away from drinking-places, are made as attractive as possible. Many acquire the habit of drinking from visiting these places, because they know they are expected to patronize the drinking saloons by drinking themselves; if they enjoy their hospitality, they must take a little alcoholic stimulus to repay them. I wish our Young Men's Christian Association, in connection with looking after the spiritual interests of the young men, would connect reading-rooms, bath-rooms, and an attractive gymnasium with their rooms; and thereby show an interest in providing suitable amusements and entertainments to draw them away from gambling-rooms and disreputable places. Many of our young men avoid religious meetings. Let us have no compulsory features about them, but make the rooms cheerful, social and free from anything wrong, but have nothing to repel the class who need them most.

On Sunday our first thought was to go and hear Spurgeon, and we were fortunate in finding him at home, and able to preach. He is suffering terribly with the gout, and is unable to preach often. His great church is in the form of an amphitheater, with two galleries extending around the entire room, in the rear as well as front of the platform, and will hold, when packed, about eight thousand. Every seat was occupied to-day, indicating some six thousand present. First come upon the platform about one hundred boys from his orphan school, and take their seats, and then follow the officers of the church. Over the platform is a high pulpit, surrounded by a railing, which Mr. Spurgeon, soon entering, occupies and commences the services at once with an earnest prayer. He is a rather short, thick-set man, and to look at him one wonders whence such great influence and power for good can come; but when he gets thoroughly warmed in his discourse, you find yourself in full sympathy with the great audience, for all around you are men and women weeping, showing that he knows how to touch human sympathies and well understands human nature. In referring to some people that were always despondent, he said: "They always squeeze the juices of sorrow out of the clusters of Eshcol." The sermon was about an hour long, and delivered entirely without notes. Earnest, eloquent, and full of beautiful expression, he was not by any means the coarse, sledge-hammer man I expected to see. After service he invited all members of churches to unite with them in celebrating the Lord's Supper in the chapel. There are about five thousand members of his church, and one of the deacons pointed out to me a poor, decrepit old lady, who was the first one on the list of church members.

In the afternoon we all went to St. Margaret's Church to hear Canon Farrar, who has, by his published sermons on eternal punishment, drawn the attention of people toward him. He is a fine-looking man. He preached a good sermon, directed mostly to young men, condemning the frivolous habits and fast lives of the young men of England who, having inherited wealth and position, yet made it a curse to them on account of their dissipation. We have heard Dr. Parker, the leading Congregational minister, and Dr. Cumming, the prominent Presbyterian clergyman, and Dr. Punshon, Methodist, and could not but feel that they are more than equaled by Bishop Simpson, Dr. Phillips Brooks of Boston, Dr. John Hall, Dr. Storrs, Beecher and others in America.

We find Americans everywhere, and in greater numbers, it is said, than ever before. Dr. Parker, I think, said to us, "You Americans, I suppose, have come over to tell us how hard the times are in America." There are so many things of interest in London that one wants at least a month to see them.

We have been here about ten days, and have not yet visited all the places of special interest, such as the Natural History Gallery, etc. We were delighted in spending a day at Kensington Museum, where, among other objects of interest, is the Forster Collection, which contains the original manuscripts of Dickens's works—Oliver Twist, Old Curiosity Shop, American Notes, Bleak House, Little Dorrit, David Copperfield, Dombey and Son, and many others. Nearly one-half, or more, of each line had been erased and re-written, showing with what care Dickens prepared his works for publication. It was very difficult for me to read them, even with a glass, and no one but printers could do it, for they seem to have a sort of intuitive power to read poor scribbling and make out what one wants to say. There are also original letters or manuscripts of William Cowper, Keats, Thomas Campbell, Samuel Johnson, Alexander Pope, Daniel De Foe, author of "Robinson Crusoe," John Locke, Sir Isaac Newton, Addison, Thomas Moore, John Hampden's letter to his friend, Sir John Elliott, at his lodging in the Tower, and many others. The collection of paintings is one of the most valuable in London, and has not been here long, but attracts great attention. The admission to this Museum is free three times a week.

We made an excursion to the environs of London. In every direction are most attractive places, none more so than Hampton Court and Richmond Hill, with its park of three thousand acres, on the bank of the Thames, thirteen miles from London. At the latter, one gets one of the finest views of the beautiful country, with London and Windsor Castle in the distance. We take a carriage and ride through Twickenham, past many delightful places occupied by lords and ladies; their names I do not care to remember. Pope's villa and Lady Russell's are the most prominent. We ride through Bushy Park, a splendid avenue of horse-chestnut trees, one mile long—the park stretching away in green glades and small lakes on either side. We see all about picnic parties enjoying the cool shade and velvety lawns, and notice some boys starting up and chasing a herd of deer. The flowers, covering the grove of horse-chestnut trees in May, are said to be a most attractive sight, filling the air with fragrance.

As we pass into the grounds connected with Hampton Court, it looks, all around us and in the distance, like a wild tract of land with immense trees, as are some of those beautiful pasture-grounds, interspersed with oak openings, in Madison County, Ohio. The day was warm, and the sun shone out brightly. The walks were delightful. Most of the English parks seem to be left as near their natural state as possible, but of late years more attention is paid to landscape gardening; and here you come suddenly upon flower-beds of every artistic shape and every bright, beautiful flower that could be imagined, arranged along the walks under the yew trees in every direction, almost as far as the eye can reach; here are arches of trees, and here flowers and lawns, and artificial lakes and water-courses, covered with water-lilies and white water-fowl; with the sober, majestic, red-brick walls of the palace, covering eight acres, in the background, and with three thousand five hundred and ninety-six acres of park in view. It presents an appearance of grandeur and beauty long to be remembered. We enter the palace, which has been occupied by nine different sovereigns. Its long suits of apartments seem to be the gathering-place of historical antiquities, paintings, old furnished parlors and dressing-rooms (the State

Bed-room among them), with the ancient beds and furniture. The whole number of pictures at Hampton Court is about one thousand. The palace garden has a vinery where there is a grape-vine over ninety years old, which has yielded three thousand bunches of black Hamburg grapes in one year. The principal stem is forty-two inches round at the base, and is over one hundred and ten feet long. We spent a whole day here, and could not but say, "In what other country could one find the same perfection of gardening?" The grass was soft and green, and the dark shade of the yew and brown beech contrasted finely with the lighter verdure of the oak and the smooth-leaved, elegant lime and rougher elm. I cannot describe the scene; it was enough to enjoy it. The palace was originally built by Cardinal Wolsey, who was also its architect. "The historian relates that at Hampton Court were two hundred and eighty beds of silk for royal and noble guests."

From these historical antiquities and old paintings, one turns with delight to the exhibition of the Royal Academy — all modern pictures. This is the one hundred and tenth exhibition, opening in May and closing on the first of August. Here are about fifteen hundred paintings and some one hundred pieces of sculpture, the list of exhibitors numbering about nine hundred. No artist is allowed to exhibit more than eight different works; none which have already been publicly exhibited in London being admitted, and no copies of any kind. The Academy was established over one hundred years ago, by George III. Its principal objects are the maintenance of a school or academy of design for gratuitous instruction of students in art, and an annual exhibition, free to all artists of distinguished merit. It is a private society, supporting a school open to the people from its own resources, without any grant of public money. The first President was Sir Joshua Reynolds. The President now [1878] is Sir Daniel McNee. Among the paintings, of course, are some of the first productions of modern art; and to me, not a connoisseur in such matters, it seemed a rich day's enjoyment to be where I could examine so many works by the artists of the later school, and judge for myself whether they were good or not. I must confess that, although many of the works by the old masters may be of rare worth, as showing the history and progress of art, yet I cannot see the merit which is often attributed to them.

However, in this I plead ignorance. The paintings were of every conceivable design. Bierstadt had one on exhibition which was much admired, entitled " Estes Park, Colorado, U. S."

We could not cross over to the Continent until we had visited the greatest bank in the world, the Bank of England, with its one thousand clerks, and its low but attractive stone buildings, covering three acres. The area in the center is planted with shrubs and ornamented with a fountain. There is a valuable library for the use of the clerks. The value of banknotes in circulation is about one hundred millions of dollars. The specie or bullion in its vaults amounts to one hundred and thirty millions of dollars. It pays interest on deposits, as do all the banks in Great Britain. The interest paid is from one to two and a half per cent. We see no bank-bills in England except the Bank of England notes, which go at par anywhere in Europe. The Bank buildings here all look old and dingy. It is said that the bankers and rich business men abhor fresh, new and showy fronts and counters for offices; but the older and more begrimed they are the better, as an indication of an Englishman's substantial character and his aversion to change. A visit to some of these old commercial houses, whose monetary transactions are counted by millions, is quite interesting. The firm that I had business with seemed to boast of having rooms for their office which had been occupied by Queen Anne Boleyn.

It is said that over eighteen hundred children are born in London every week, and that there are over twelve hundred deaths.

We leave now for the Continent, feeling that we have had a hurried, and therefore somewhat unsatisfactory visit.

VIII.

EMINENT BRITISH DIVINES*....PUNSHON...PULSFORD....
WILBERFORCE.

London.

WE have heard in Great Britain eight notable preachers — Punshon, Pulsford, Wilberforce, Parker, Cumming, Farrar, Stanley and Spurgeon. I will now give you my impressions of the first three, reserving the remaining five for my next letter.

Dr. W. Morley Punshon was in Dublin on Sunday, June 23d (a day which we spent there), in attendance upon the M. E. Conference of Ireland. He preached in the "large Concert Hall" of the International

---

*The present letter and the following one were kindly furnished by Rev. R. G. Hutchins, D. D., Pastor of the First Congregational Church, Columbus, Ohio, who is my pastor, and who was my traveling companion during the pleasant journeyings of which the present volume is the record.

Exhibition Palace of 1853—a hall which, with its wings, will seat between three and four thousand people. The service was to commence at half-past three o'clock P. M., and before three o'clock the entrances were thronged with people. We found the hall literally packed; for be it known unto you that Dr. Punshon is generally esteemed by his denomination in Great Britain as their most eloquent preacher.

Barely room enough for the speaker was left on the stage by the time of his arrival. He is a large-framed, heavy man, perfectly erect, with full, red face and dark-brown curly hair, which is wanting on the top of the head. He is perhaps fifty years old. Over his eyes, which are half hidden with flesh, he wears spectacles, at least when reading. His whole appearance and bearing suggest solidity and power. He might sit for the portrait of the typical Englishman. A few years since, his face and style were made familiar to many American audiences. You will remember that he served two years in Canada for his deceased wife's sister, whom he could not, according to English law, marry at home. The term of his service was vastly more reasonable than that which Rachel's father exacted from Jacob. Two of his lectures in America

— one upon "Daniel," the other upon "The Huguenots"—I heard in Brooklyn. They were too highly wrought—the "tool-marks" were too apparent —to be received with enthusiasm in a country where Mr. Beecher's naturalness and spontaneity have so largely set the fashion for oratory. But he evidently improved his time among us, studying our history and visiting our national shrines; for I observed that he was advertised in the Dublin papers for a lecture, on the Wednesday evening following his sermon, upon "The Men of the Mayflower." I saw a report of this lecture, as previously delivered, which proved, concerning Plymouth Rock, that he "*had been there.*"

He commenced and continued his discourse in a natural, straightforward way, like a man having a direct, honest purpose. His voice was too high and loud at the beginning, and was unduly sustained in pitch and volume throughout. It sounds as if it had been strained. Blunt, familiar sentences were occasionally interjected, but the bulk of the discourse was highly elaborate and ornate. His imagination is tropical in its luxuriance, and as he takes you through his tangled forest-paths and bowers of beauty you sometimes begin to doubt his earnestness, and to question whether it may not be his chief purpose to show you his rhetorical plantation rather than to lead you to any moral destination. But, suddenly, at the most unexpected point, you are brought out into the plain highway again, and he utters a few sentences, short and pointed, like the inscription on a guide-post, and you blame yourself for having distrusted your guide. There is a striking contrast between the man's ponderous frame and his fine and often exquisite rhetoric. The presence of the strong man always redeems his nicety from mere prettiness.

He spoke without notes, yet it was evident that (with the exception of occasional sentences, intended to break the excessive smoothness of the flow of his polished periods) the sermon had been carefully written and committed to memory. His text was Mat. 5: 14, 15, 16: "Ye are the light of the world," etc. The following were his three grand heads:

1. "Light is derived, and therefore humble. It is not ye but your light that is to shine."

2. "Light is self-evidencing, and therefore cannot be hid. Does any one ever ask if you are a Christian? Then you are no proper Christian at all. Did any one ask where Moses had been when he descended

from the Mount with the glory of God shining in his face?"

3. "Light is a pleasant thing, and therefore needs no apology."

Here he enumerated some of the substantial reasons for Christian joy. Shall I jot down for you a few of his sentences as specimens? "Christians are to let their light shine, not as hermits but as men; not in the convent, but in the company." "The primary duty of the Christian is to glorify God—to fill life with doxologies of song and hallelujahs of service." "When duty, with solitary finger, points one way, and self-interest and the applause of men point the other, the Christian obeys the index of God." "The Christian is to let his light shine before men; he is not to glare it upon them as a policeman suddenly glares his lantern upon the affrighted criminal." "The path of the just shines dimmer and dimmer? No, that is the class-meeting version of it. No, brighter and brighter!" "Naturalists tell us that the eye of the eagle droops and weeps when it looks at the sun. The world has an eagle eye for your faults; but let your light shine so purely that its critical eye shall droop before the brightness and beauty of your life."

Having heard Morley Punshon twice, and also read a volume of his published discourses, I am sure I should not expect from his preaching, with all its excellences, any of those mighty works which accompanied and followed that of the illustrious founder of Methodism.

In Glasgow we heard Dr. William Pulsford, a Congregationalist, who is accounted one of the two or three first preachers in the city. He is said to have the faculty of attracting and holding young men. He is a small man, rather frail than robust in appearance, with a high forehead and thin, study-worn face, and is about sixty years of age. His manner is exceedingly quiet and conversational. His thoughts are clean-cut and distinct. His sentences are concise and rich-freighted. He is not fluent; continuity is broken by too long pauses between passages. His language is classical in its purity, and yet impresses you not as the result of present effort or special preparation—not as the treading of the wine-press, but as the bursting juice from the ripe clusters of culture. Though deep, rich sweetness and purity chiefly characterized his discourse, yet it was not without passages of real power. I heard him spoken of as a popular preacher, but, judging from the sermon I heard, I should never venture to call him one.

There is no living Scotchman whom I so much desired to hear as Prof. John Caird, who now holds a chair in the University of Glasgow, and seldom preaches. His present manner is described as calm, and his sermons as thoughtful and scholarly, but in his earlier years he must have had an impassioned eloquence nothing less than marvelous.

We had come to Glasgow a few years too late to hear that great and good man Norman Macleod, but it was pleasant to hear his praises spoken on every hand. I am told that his likeness adorns the walls, not only of rich mansions, but also of multitudes of cottages in Highland hamlets. When the poor saw him they blessed him, and the Queen delighted in him.

We visited his church, "The Old Barony," the place where he had power with God and with men, and prevailed. It is situated in an unfashionable and even poor part of the city, near the Infirmary; yet, as the old parish church, it still enjoys a certain prestige. On the outer wall of this sanctuary we saw a permanent announcement of services "for people in working clothes." You saw at a glance that the interior of the church, with its amplitude of space and its semicircular pews, was designed for popular audiences. The people who were gathering for evening worship were of the humbler sort, and the contribution receivers in the vestibule were loaded, not with sovereigns or shillings, but pennies.

We went to hear Dr. Donald Macleod, the biographer of his famous brother, his successor as editor of *Good Words*, and one of Her Majesty's chaplains, but he was away upon his vacation. His church is in a fashionable quarter of the town, and is said to be attended by what are known in Great Britain as "the best people." We subsequently made his acquaintance on the steamboat from Oban to Inverness, and still later enjoyed a stroll with him and his brother-in-law, Rev. Dr. Clerk, the parish minister at Corpach. Through their courtesy we passed a delightful evening at the parsonage, a refined Highland home, where we heard the old Scotch ballads beautifully sung by the daughters of Dr. Clerk, assisted by their uncle, Dr. Macleod, who has a superb voice.

Professor Hoppin, of Yale, calls York Minster "the grandest building in Great Britain, and among the finest in the world." It was in the choir of this minster that we heard Canon Wilberforce, a son of Bishop Wilberforce, and grandson of the great emancipator. He is a tall, slim man, with a fine, unwhiskered face, and is about forty years old. At the beginning of his sermon you are annoyed by his high, unnatural voice and declamatory tone. He uses no gesticulation, but betrays the intensity of his temperament by his constant stepping from side to side of the little pulpit, or "theological tub." But you are soon made to forget his infelicities by the simplicity of his rhetoric and his profound earnestness. Though he reads closely, yet he makes the impression that he is doing nothing for display, but is simply seeking to press home his thoughts upon the minds and hearts of his hearers. He had come up from Southampton, where he resides, to attend the meetings of a temperance society to be held in York during the week; and, as was natural, he preached upon Temperance.

He is erecting a memorial church in honor of his father, the Bishop, one portion of which is to be built with the contributions of temperance people alone. The collection of the morning was devoted to that purpose.

His discourse was one of the boldest and grandest I have ever heard upon the subject. I have heard men preach, both at home and abroad, whose world of thought seemed infinitely removed from the *real* world of men and women, with its wants and woes, its struggles and defeats; and it did my heart good to hear a man, especially one of aristocratic prestige and in an aristocratic place, speak as if he really knew something of the sins and sorrows of the teeming masses outside of church walls, who are, alas! too often outside, also, of the bounds of our sympathy and effort. The services which we had attended in English cathedrals had not prepared us to expect, in such a quarter, a sermon like that of Canon Wilberforce.

At one cathedral choral service we counted three ecclesiastics, seven men and twelve boy singers, one organist and one organ-blower, and one verger— total, *twenty-five persons*,—all to edify an audience of *seven*, including ourselves and other tourists who had happened in, and one little boy. The intoning was above criticism, and the service was artistically rendered, but I could not help saying (and may the dear Lord forgive me if I was uncharitable) that if the world is to be converted by such means, the accomplishment of the work must be indefinitely postponed. No part of that choral service seemed more in keeping with the hour than the petition "that we may spend our time in rest and quietness," which petition seemed to be richly answered in the case of the celebrants.

Canon Wilberforce, taking total-abstinence ground in the presence of a beer and wine bibbing congregation, illustrated the law of heredity, exhibiting the courage which dwelt in his grandfather, the statesman, and his father, the Bishop, and, I am persuaded, in himself also. Repeatedly the ancestral fire flamed out. He quoted statistics showing the relation of the great recent increase of crime and pauperism to intemperance. The present depression of business, and consequent dissatisfaction of the working classes, he thought largely due to the withdrawal of such vast amounts of money and so much enterprise from legitimate channels, to supply the self-indulgent drinking habits of the people.

In a most impressive and pathetic passage, he illustrated the damage inflicted by drink upon domestic life. He spoke from his own observation, and told of "one of the gentlest and most devoted wives he ever knew, over whose grave the earth is scarcely set, who, having borne with a drunken, brutal husband for long years, received from him a kick which liberated her anguish-stricken spirit, and suffered it to fly where the wicked cease from troubling and the weary are at rest; while her babe, prematurely born, lay dead by the dead mother's side." While reciting at her funeral the blessed words of the burial service, he had vowed never to cease lifting up his voice against the vice by which that woman had been murdered.

The wonderful *ring* of the sermon may be guessed from two or three sentences which are printed on my memory. Speaking of the impossibility of restraining men's lusts by law, he said: "This is not the platform; and yet, before this altar, I declare that there is nothing at which the devils laugh more than at an act of Parliament." Again: "The Church of England of to-day, with its polished and gilded formalism, is pining for want of zeal. Christ can bear with our *opposition* better than our *indifference*. 'I would ye were even either cold or hot.'" These words sounded heroic in the choir of York Minster. Everything considered, nothing which I have heard on this side the water has moved me like this sermon by Canon Wilberforce.

I can close this letter with no more cheering news than that the temperance cause is advancing wonderfully in Great Britain. Four of the Bishops of the Church of England and three of the Canons of Westminster, including Canon Farrar, are now total abstainers, and are outspoken in defense of their principles. The Duke of Westminster, who is accounted the richest man in the country, is also using his vast influence in favor of temperance, though I do not understand that he has yet taken the total abstinence ground. So much for progress among the powers that be. Meanwhile, Mr. William Noble, who commenced public speaking as a reformed drunkard by repeating from memory parts of Mr. Gough's lectures, has been over to the United States and learned the methods of the "Murphy movement," and introduced them in one of the worst quarters of London. The reformed men are called the "Blue Ribbon Army," and the Murphy pledge is most solemnly administered. The meetings are held in the "Hoxton Music Hall," a place where low concerts were formerly given, and which was closed by the police as a disreputable place. I attended one of these meetings, and I confess that I never before saw so motley a crowd. They poured in fresh from the slums. The evening was the one hundred and tenth night that the meetings had been held, and four thousand five hundred signers to the pledge had been secured.

IX.

Dr. Joseph Parker....Dr. John Cumming....Canon Farrar....Dean Stanley....Charles H. Spurgeon.

London.

DR. JOSEPH PARKER, of London, is known to Americans through his published works, especially his " Ecce Deus." Many of our countrymen made his personal acquaintance at the meeting of the Evangelical Alliance in New York, in 1873, where he delivered an admirable address upon " Modern Preaching and its Requirements." His appointment to this service, on so important an occasion, indicates the rank he has attained in his art. Occasional copies of his weekly paper, *The Fountain*, which publishes his sermons, find their way across the sea.

We heard one of his Thursday-noon discourses to business men. His church edifice is conveniently situated for such mid-week services, being near a business center. The sermons which he gives on these occasions have all been previously delivered to his Sabbath congregations.

Dr. Parker is a large-framed, bulky man, with black hair and eyes, and a broad, full, red face. His bearing and speech betoken great self-reliance, an imperious will, force and energy, and no small self-complacency. His first utterances in our hearing were those of prayer, and suggested self-consciousness and an affected loftiness. His sermon was delivered entirely without notes, and was characterized by strength, fluency, beauty and unction. He proved himself a master of sarcasm and irony, and of pathos as well. He won and held the warm sympathy of his hearers. They smiled, they wept, were instructed and convinced. Before the benediction, the preacher announced that *The Fountain* for the week contained the sermon to which we had just listened, and would be for sale in the vestibule. So, many of us had the sermon both *given* to us and *sold* to us, and thus preserved two copies, one on "the fleshly tables of the heart," the other on "the printed page."

Though Dr. Parker is a man of recognized power, yet conservative Londoners speak of him as sensational. And, certainly, not all his measures for attracting the public ear and eye would seem delicate, even to our less fastidious American taste. This fear haunted me in hearing him, that he had more *ability* than *amiability*.

One Sunday afternoon we attended Crown Court Chapel, near Covent Garden, London, and were surprised to find a congregation of only some fifty persons, where admiring throngs were wont to gather. The pastor, Dr. John Cumming, a minister of the Scottish Church, and a Scotchman by birth, is a tall, well-proportioned, refined and venerable old gentleman, about seventy years of age. He has, as you know, been a voluminous theological writer, a distinguished adversary of the Romish Church, and a steadfast opponent of the party which, under Chalmers, founded the Free Church of Scotland.

His sermon (if a disjointed talk upon a variety of subjects, having no relevancy to the text, deserves so considerable a name) was an abundant explanation of the empty pews. He read, apparently from a little commonplace book, thoughts which had not the remotest mutual kinship; lifting his eyes between the passages and proceeding to thin them down by extemporaneous remarks. In his prime he is said to have had "a peerless capacity for continuousness," which he still retains. But the old-time delight of his hearers has given place to a patient, respectful weariness. The spectacle was altogether pitiable. But our hearts were melted in tender sympathy for him when we subsequently learned that the career of a reckless son had broken down the noble old man more than the weight of years.

His style of speaking has always been fluent and conversational. Though never among the strongest and grandest of preachers, yet his was formerly a genuine and captivating eloquence, and for grace and polish of manner he was unsurpassed.

Canon Farrar is apparently about forty-five years old. He is of medium height and neither fleshy nor thin, but plump and well rounded. His brain is probably never dull nor dizzy from plethora, neither is he haunted by dyspeptic horrors. He seems like a man in thoroughly sound health. He has a large, symmetrical head, round in its general form and partially bald, with a high, broad forehead. His hair is dark brown and his eyes are small. He is erect in form, having nothing of the "scholarly stoop" which we naturally associate with the writer of many books. You would call him a fine-looking man. He has not attained entire self-possession or self-forgetfulness in public address, but his face is red with blushes.

We heard him in St. Margaret's Chapel, which stands within the inclosure of Westminster Abbey. He is much discussed just now on account of his recent deliverances upon the doctrine of future punishment, and his photograph is conspicuous in the book-shop windows. We therefore anticipated finding a crowded house, but there were seats for many who had staid away.

His sermon was about what his published discourses had prepared me to look for. It was exceptionally clear and pure in language, but sufficiently commonplace in thought. It was a contrast between Samuel and the sons of Eli. He spoke some words of denunciation concerning the dissipation of young men belonging to the gentry and nobility, which, from the sensation they caused, were evidently regarded as bold; and in all his utterances there breathed a high, free and manly spirit; but in no sentence did he exhibit great power or impressiveness. Farrar reads closely, and his tones in delivery are execrable—the inevitable sing-song of the English Church.

In one part of his sermon he betrayed annoyance and hesitancy, which culminated in a pause, followed by the remark: "We do not wish people to come here who are not willing to remain through the services." By which it appears that some had come to hear the superb music, and, not being spellbound by the preacher, were retiring. Thus it seems that even a Canon may not be a sufficiently big gun to carry all before him.

It is not strange that the English Church, though she develops the ablest and most scholarly men, is not rich in great preachers. The ritual and not the sermon is emphasized. If comparatively little is expected from the sermon, it is natural that comparatively little should be done for it. Moreover,

DEAN STANLEY.

the splendid prizes, in place and titles, with which the Church rewards superior authorship, successfully invite time and strength from pulpit preparation. The widow and biographer of Charles Kingsley says that "his sermons were always remarkable." But he who turns from "Hypatia" or "Alton Locke" to read Kingsley's discourses, cannot fail to conclude that the press rather than the pulpit claimed and got the lion's share of the thought and labor of that knightly soul. Those who have been instructed and charmed by the scholarly and delightful books of Farrar are doomed to some degree of disappointment when they hear him preach.

Of Dean Stanley it may be said, more truly, perhaps, than of any other minister of the Church of England, that he is the bright, consummate flower of the highest English breeding and culture. The son of the Bishop of Norwich, he was a pupil of Arnold, of Rugby, and subsequently his biographer. A graduate of Oxford, he became Regius Professor of Ecclesiastical History in that University. Chaplain to Prince Albert, he became the intimate and beloved friend of Her Majesty the Queen, who gave him one of the noblest and best of the ladies of her court in marriage. He was selected to accompany the Prince of Wales in his journey through the East, which tour furnished Stanley the raw materials for his rich and vivid volume upon Sinai and Palestine. And now he wears his crowning honors as Dean of Westminster; and, despite his splendid career, wonderful to relate, he holdeth fast his integrity! He is said to be simple and child-like in manner and spirit.

We heard him preach, in his own cathedral, probably his last sermon before his visit to America. Every seat and standing-place within reach of his voice was occupied, and he was listened to with profound and sympathetic attention.

He is a short, slim man, with head and shoulders slightly bent. He is now sixty-three years old, but he seems much older, his voice and whole appearance suggesting feebleness. He is, however, evidently in poor health. His face has great delicacy of mould, and a serious, refined and gentle expression. His eye is light, probably blue, and his hair and English side beard are thoroughly bleached. His fine head and fair forehead betoken the predominance of intellect. You see at a glance that he is a fine-fibered man.

He reads his sermon closely, without changing his position or making a gesture. Nothing favorable to his elocution can be said, except that there is evident warmth and sympathy in his voice, and a rhythm in his tones in curious keeping with the rhythm of his sentences, and really interpreting their thought. In themselves considered, his inflections are absurd; but, sustaining the flow of his noble rhetoric, and conveying to the ear his generous meaning, we welcome them for what they bring. He who presents us with pearls in a rich casket may be shabbily dressed; but, in the light of his gift, we are ready to make oath that he is "clothed in purple and fine linen."

Stanley's sermon was upon Elijah at Horeb: and, after hearing it, I turned to his "Jewish Church," and found several passages which he had, "for substance of doctrine," reproduced, and others which he had almost literally reproduced. Though birth and privilege and royal favor have raised him to a position far above the masses of men, yet he evidently lives in the same world with them, and sympathizes with their aspirations, their struggles and discouragements. The discourse was full of hope and charity—the helping hand of a valiant brother.

How beautiful a thing is genuine culture! Such culture is, I think, always recognized by two tokens,—self-restraint and orderliness. The uncultivated but hospitable housewife places before her guests viands excessive in variety and quality, with defective taste in arrangement and manner of serving. But the refined housewife shows her breeding in the restraining hand, and in the order and delicacy of her table. An uncultivated speaker is in danger of overcrowding his address, and presenting his thoughts in a crude, mixed way. But a ripe scholar, like Stanley, does not attempt to give too much, but presents the thoughts he offers clearly, strongly, elegantly.

Moreover, this must be said of Dean Stanley, that however much you may differ from him in doctrinal or ecclesiastical views, you must admire and love this man, who has evidently got past Esek, the well of strife and controversy, and beyond Sitnah, the well of recrimination, even to Rehoboth, the place of largeness and breadth.

I have heard Mr. Spurgeon three times—twice in 1858, and now again in 1878. I first heard him

REV. C. H. SPURGEON.

at Epsom Race-course, where the celebrated Derby races are run. The race season had passed, and he spoke for the benefit of a church there (an admission-fee being charged), in the grand stand of the course. His text was 1. Cor. ix. 24: "Know ye not, that they which run in a race, run all, but one receiveth the prize? So run, that ye may obtain." I took no notes of the sermon, but the points he made can never fade from my memory. These were his heads: I. "*No horse runs in the race that is not entered.*" From which he inferred the necessity of having one's name enrolled in the Lamb's Book of Life, and an actual entrance upon the Christian course, in order to a successful ending of the race. II. "*No horse wins in the race that is heavily laden,*" and here he urged the necessity of laying aside every weight, etc. III. "*No horse wins in the race that leaps the posts and rails, and gets out of the course entirely.*" From which he predicted the failure of such Christian professors as go over to profane *isms* and practices. IV. "*No horse wins in the race that stops to kick his competitors.*"

At this time Spurgeon was but twenty-four years old, and had been preaching in London four years.

The following Sunday I heard him in Surrey Music Hall, and though an admission fee of a shilling was charged, to feed the fund for building the Metropolitan Chapel, the house seemed full of paying auditors before the doors were opened to the non-paying crowd. But *then* the people poured in like the sea when the dikes are leveled.

Even at this early period of his ministry he spoke with the same assurance and self-possession which now characterize him. The consciousness of his embassadorship led him, even in extreme youth, to speak "as one having authority, and not as the scribes." A friend of mine, who heard him when he was but eighteen years old, at which age he became pastor of a church at Waterbeach, testifies that when, at the close of his discourse, he appealed to the aged, they were deeply moved, the whole air of the preacher indicating his right to counsel and warn his grey-haired seniors. He brought the expectation of doing a great work in the ministry up with him from childhood. His father and grandfather were both independent ministers, and on one occasion, when Richard Knill was visiting the latter in Essex, the good missionary took Charles, then a little, white-haired lad, into the garden, and talked with him awhile under a yew-tree. After praying with him, he took the boy upon his knee and said: "This child will preach the gospel, and he will preach it to the largest congregations of our times." In one of his published sermons Mr. Spurgeon thus refers to this utterance of Mr. Knill: "I believed," says Spurgeon, "his prophecy, and my standing here to-day is partly occasioned by such belief. It did not hinder me in my diligence in seeking to educate myself because I believed I was destined to preach to large congregations; not at all; but the prophecy helped forward its own fulfillment; and I prayed and sought and strove, always having this star of Bethlehem before me, that the day should come when I should preach the gospel."

On his first appearance in London, and for several years afterward, many regarded him as a mushroom growth, and he was harshly criticised and even ridiculed. But his influence as a preacher and pastor and organizer have yearly increased, even to this day. His average congregation numbers from five to six thousand, and he has, on occasions, preached to an assembly of twenty-five thousand people. His sermons are translated into all the principal European languages. His training college furnishes scores of preachers every Sabbath, from among its students, for the destitute sections of the metropolis, and its graduates are eagerly sought by Baptist churches throughout England. His earnest, evangelical, catholic spirit has elevated the tone of the churches of his order throughout the United Kingdom.

If I were asked to summarize Mr. Spurgeon's elements of power, I could not fail to mention: 1. A voice of wonderful clearness, sweetness and compass. 2. Marvelous fluency. 3. Perfect self-possession. 4. Great variety of thought and illustration. 5. The habit of distributing his thought under pointed and concise heads. 6. Robust common-sense, bringing him into sympathy with the common people, who always hear him gladly. 7. Profound sincerity and earnestness.

Of this last-mentioned characteristic, Henry Vincent, the English orator, gave me an illustration. Mr. Vincent, having been impressed by a simple presentation of the truth by Mr. Spurgeon, repaired to the ante-room after service, to thank him for the sermon. The door was ajar, and the preacher was leaning his head upon his hand in the attitude of prayer. Lifting his eyes, he warmly welcomed his visitor. "I did not intend to intrude," said Mr. Vincent, "but simply wanted to express my enjoyment of your sermon." "But they will so soon forget it! They will so soon forget it!" exclaimed Mr. Spurgeon, while the tears were rolling down his cheeks.

In personal conversation, this pastor of the Metropolitan Tabernacle exhibits, in the most delightful way, the simplicity, frankness, warmth and kindness of his nature.

Suffering now from the gout, he has to spend, every year, some months (and those the most propitious for Christian work) away from the moist climate of England, usually in Italy. This annual season of exile he regards as one of the severest trials of his life.

When we remember the immense size of his weekly congregations and the variety and efficiency of the benevolent agencies of his church, and estimate the far-reaching influence of his published discourses, and the personal power of his hundreds of living epistles in the pulpits of the land; and when we bring to mind the prominence of his position in the midst of the largest and wealthiest capital of Europe; and when, moreover, we recollect that the man who has been the inspirer and mainspring of all this wonderful and far-reaching system of benefactions, not for a year but for a quarter of a century, is but forty-four years old, we need not hesitate to declare that the career of Charles H. Spurgeon is unparalleled in the history of the Christian church.

X.

FROM LONDON TO PARIS....FIRST IMPRESSIONS OF THE FRENCH METROPOLIS....THE SECOND GREAT EXPOSITION....THE TUILERIES, THE TROCADERO, AND SURROUNDINGS....AMERICA'S EDUCATIONAL EXHIBIT.... COLUMBUS IN THE GREAT EXPOSITION.

Paris.

OUR trip from London to Calais was a pleasant one, twenty-four miles by rail to Dover, through a thriving country of towns, interspersed with green fields and grain and hops. We took the new double steamer "Calais-Doveres" across the usually boisterous British Channel, which was as smooth and calm as one could wish. This new steamer looks like two lashed together, and will run just as well backward as forward. Indeed, it has no stern; it has two prows at each end, and the paddle-wheels are in the center. The construction is to prevent its rolling on this stormy sea. This was the first time it had been used for a passenger steamer, though once it had brought over Lord Beaconsfield from the Berlin Congress. He was received with great enthusiasm in London while we were there. He seems to be exceedingly popular with the English people, and almost every Englishman that we conversed with lauds him to the skies and depreciates Gladstone. As we arrive and pass through France, we notice that there are no hedges or fences to divide one farm from another, and that the stock feeding upon the fields is guarded by women or children to keep them in the lots appropriated to them.

On reaching Calais we hear nothing but the French language, which is sufficiently musical when used by educated persons, especially by ladies, as they meet in social intercourse. They are so polite, and utter so many words of commendation, and do everything with so much grace, that one is inclined to be a little rude and stare at them with delight; but the jabber of the crowds seems like that of an excited mob, so many words are employed to express a little, and the people are so demonstrative.

The railroad cars—or coaches as they are called *(voitures de chemin de fer)*—look like Hawkes' stage-coaches. They are made in compartments, like the English coaches, holding in each compartment eight or ten persons, one-half riding backward. We are locked in, and off we go.

Paris is about ten hours' ride from London, all by rail except the one hour and a half by steamer across the Channel. Everybody says that "Paris is the most beautiful city in the world." As we get up in the morning and take our first walk up the Boulevard d'Opera and Rue de Rivoli, to the new Opera House, and notice the long blocks of handsome, cream-colored stone buildings, with mansard roofs, and the clean asphalt pavements, the artistic windows filled with beautiful goods of every description, and walk up and down the splendid boulevards (of which there are over seventeen hundred), with their fine shade-trees, one can enjoy them with a zest in comparison with the dingy, old-looking buildings in London. Paris used to be a fortified city. The walls and towers were pulled down, and a road made over them and planted with trees, to which the name *boulevard* (bulwark) was given.

The city was founded so far back in the past that when anything is spoken of as being "old," it must refer to something that existed or occurred before the time of Christ. Paris is proud of her palaces, monuments, fountains, parks and boulevards. While many of her monarchs have expended immense sums in improving and adorning the city, Napoleon III. did what neither Paris nor any other capital of Europe ever witnessed before in the way of improvements. He has remodeled and restored every building that was defective. Superb thoroughfares were opened. He constructed new bridges and made them free to the public, and to him more than to any one else is due the credit of making Paris the most attractive city in the world. It contains thirty-five monumental and eighty-eight unadorned fountains, besides over two thousand water-plugs, which are turned on daily to purify the streets. The drinking-fountains, which are seen everywhere, were erected through the liberality of Sir Richard Wallace. The population of Paris is two millions, and one-quarter of the births are illegitimate. As we go through the city, here and there may be seen marks of the destruction of many of her most beautiful and attractive public buildings during the Franco-Prussian war and the reign of the Commune. Many of these, however, have been rebuilt, and Paris now makes a splendid appearance, and indicates a wonderfully recuperative power in being able to duplicate the glories of 1867 in her second great Exposition on the Champ de Mars. The present Exposition was decided upon by a decree of the President of the Republic (MacMahon) in 1876, and the Commissioners determined that it should be held within the limits of the city of Paris, and the Champ de Mars was selected. It is about a mile and a half from the Grand Opera House, which is considered to be about the center of the city, and is easily reached by steamer, railroad or omnibus. Starting for the Exposition, we took the little steamer on the Seine, in front of the Tuileries; fare only twenty centimes, or four cents.

No edifice in Paris is so rich in historical associations as the Tuileries, and none, with the exception of the Hotel de Ville (City Hall), has ever been overtaken by so terrible a fate. The Communists, in 1871, aware of their desperate position and impending destruction, determined, at one of their secret meetings, to wreak their revenge on the ill-fated city by setting all the principal buildings on fire. The whole of the western side of the palace, facing the Jardin des Tuileries, and the pavilion on the north side, next to the Rue de Rivoli, were reduced to a gigantic heap of smouldering ruins, after burning three days and nights. The restoration is rapidly approaching completion, and the imposing mass of buildings forming the old and new Louvre will soon be as grand and beautiful as ever. We pass the Hotel de Ville, which remains as a monument of the terrible destruction that overtook it in those sad days of the Commune, the loss to Paris being irreparable, the library and so many public documents having been destroyed.

We see upon the right, a little further on, a splendid palace, in a style of architecture wonderfully characteristic of French genius, which is called the Trocadero. It is said to be the finest specimen of architecture in the world, and is now used as a museum for the Exposition, and is to remain permanently, to be used by the city of Paris for public festivities, etc. It is on a high elevation, and as one crosses the bridge and passes through the

THE TROCADERO.

beautiful park, a most attractive panorama is presented to the eye, replete with marvels imitative of ancient art and modern suggestion. Around are miniature lakes and cascades, fountains and flower-beds. The grounds facing the Champ de Mars were once the garden of a convent; the building, on its elevated plateau, is now an annex of the Exposition, the central portion forming an immense amphitheater, seating eight thousand people.

Before the grand pavilion is the monumental cascade, the water of which, after passing over an arched grotto, descends, by a series of marble steps, to an immense basin, ornamented with fountains and with animals representing the four quarters of the globe. When these fountains are playing in the afternoon, and scattering the spray, arched with rainbows, in every direction, nothing can be more charming. We visit the immense underground aquarium, covered with rock work, and descend by rustic stone steps, as if entering a cave; and then, winding around, we come across great plates of glass in the sides of the cave, behind which can be seen many species of fish, swimming about in their element, so arranged that they cannot see us while we gaze upon them. The length of this aquarium must be from two to three hundred feet, and it was amusing to see the excitable French people gesticulating and chattering as they passed from one section to another.

The galleries of the Trocadero, extending right and left, contain a retrospective exhibition of the products of every period of history, from the remotest times; giving a record of the progress of art and industry in their development, from the flint period down to the present day.

The main building, on the opposite side of the Seine, covers about seventy acres, and is of iron and glass, with an immense dome in the center and at each of the four corners. It is not a success in an architectural point of view; but for the purposes for which it was designed nothing could be better adapted. The ground upon which the Exhibition is held covers upward of one hundred and fifty acres, and everything is most admirably combined and arranged. Passing through the grand halls, we are amazed at the rich display of everything useful and ornamental — the choicest and best that every nation on the globe can produce (except the United States).

The first object that meets the eye is the unique India palace or temple, in which are the presents received by the Prince of Wales while in India, embracing every variety of precious stones and rich productions which that country can offer. To possess these would be a fortune alone. Then we come upon the Gobelin tapestry and "Sevres" porcelain vases, etc. These are from the national manufactories, which are conducted by the French government, and none of the goods are sold. No expense and pains have been spared by the government to make this display superior to any other in the world, and one needs weeks to enjoy and properly appreciate it. The French National Regalia, valued at from fifteen to twenty millions of dollars, comes next, all diamonds and precious stones, and they seem almost as large and plentiful as pebbles upon the sea-shore. Eugenie's diamond necklace is three feet long, with large diamonds glittering and sparkling like so many stars. The Regent (a solitaire) is shown, which I should think would measure one and a half by one and three-quarter inches. There are necklaces of diamonds, emeralds, sapphires, rubies and opals combined, tempting a lover of the beautiful to break the command against covetousness; also Napoleon's sword, with the hilt of solid diamonds, all making a display of precious stones not equaled in the world.

The buildings containing the exhibits of the different nations front upon the Rue des Nations, down which we now pass. As specimens characteristic of the respective styles of architecture of the different countries of the world, they are, in chasteness and elegance of design, a study and a wonder. Japan shows a small Buddhist temple; the Chinese adopt a style of building characteristic of the Celestial empire; Spain, of Moorish architecture; Persia, Tunis and Morocco present a beautiful minaret. Says a French writer, "The façade of the United States building is one of those wooden structures which the settlers of the interior erect." I hope not, if Ohio is in the interior. It is a showy, gilded-looking building, covered all over with shields. On these shields are emblazoned the coats of arms of the thirteen original States, and also that of the District of Columbia. The building would attract attention, certainly, but by no means represents our style of architecture. We should call it altogether too

"Frenchy." We could not, however, pass without taking off our hats to the old flag, with its stars and stripes floating in the breeze.

Here is a grand opportunity to study the productions in art, science and industry of England, France, Spain, Italy, Sweden, Norway, Russia, China, Turkey, and, indeed, of every nation on the globe. Though ignorant of their different tongues, we can enjoy and appreciate the wonderful results of the unceasing progress of the world, as represented here.

Naturally, we first find ourselves in the exhibit of the United States. Here everything looks bright and active, and indicates at least our "go-aheaditiveness." There are but eleven or twelve hundred exhibits from the United States, although, considering our capacity and genius, we ought to have had a representation worthy of the Great Republic; but the dilatoriness and stinginess of Congress in the matter have deprived us in a measure of a grand opportunity. The educational exhibit is one of the most important features of the American section. Two very appropriate mottoes have been chosen for the outer wall of the pavilion — Montesquieu's famous maxim, "*C'est dans le gouvernment republicain que l'on a besoin de toute la paissance de l'education,*" and the sage saying of Washington, "Promote, as an object of primary importance, institutions for the general diffusion of knowledge"; and as you enter the room you notice prominently this motto, "Public instruction is free in every State in the Union." Every American feels proud of this, and the common people of all other nations applaud it. We may well pride ourselves upon our educational exhibit, which, notwithstanding the great drawback of lack of space, has attracted general notice and admiration. It is said to be fuller and more perfect than that of any other nation, except, of course, France herself, who has a wide stretch of halls at her disposal to spread out an exhibit scarcely more important than ours, which could well cover ten times the ground it occupies at present. A supplementary educational exhibition is to be held in the Palais Royale, where the United States has been invited to make an exhibit; and France or Paris (I did not understand which) has appropriated one hundred thousand francs to bear the expenses of teachers who have been selected, for their reputation in their respective departments, to come to the exhibition from all parts of France; each one is to make a report of their observations, and their head-quarters to be in the hall of the Palais Royale occupied by the United States. This will give us an opportunity to show our resources in this department, the superintendent of which is assured that we shall take many awards, notwithstanding our poor opportunity for display. Our exhibit of national education is a great and gratifying success. The French have adopted a number of our educational methods, and recognize our superiority in all practical branches, though, of course, in everything that appertains to art they are masters of the world.

What the United States does exhibit shows that we have sacrificed the beautiful to the useful to a certain extent, and in this respect the character of our department is different from that of other nations, whose strong point is art rather than science and industry. In agricultural machinery I have no doubt we shall take the principal awards. I notice around the exhibit of Fay & Co., of Cincinnati, of "wood-working machinery," an interested crowd, while the machinery is highly commended. In passing through the department of agricultural tools I noticed a fine display, attractively arranged. On looking up to see where they were from, I read as follows, from a gilt-lettered sign: "Brown, Hinman & Co., Dayton, Ohio." I always supposed that this enterprising firm was located in Columbus. The Ohio Tool Company, of Columbus, make a creditable display of carpenters' hand tools. The Revolving Scraper Company show their scraper in a prominent place, and the Lechner Mining Machine Company exhibit one of their coal-mining machines, which is attracting a good deal of attention. These were all the exhibits I saw from Columbus.

XI.

FINE ART DEPARTMENT OF THE EXPOSITION....NOTABLE WORKS BY AMERICAN ARTISTS....ART AS AN EDUCATOR ....PARIS AND PHILADELPHIA....HOTEL LIFE....THE FRENCH SABBATH.

Paris.

THE Fine Art Galleries of the Exposition are beautifully arranged, and are as if you entered a large and splendid palace with numerous halls and parlors. As you pass from one to the other you observe that the walls are tastefully hung with paintings, the floors carpeted and the doorways handsomely draped with curtains, while over each is the name of the country it represents. It is an enchanting scene. Here are the choicest and rarest productions of living modern artists. France has the greatest number of paintings, two thousand and seventy-one in all, while the United States has only one hundred and twenty-six. France will of course take the first awards. She has a number of distinguished artists, and Meissonier, the most famous of all, has twenty pictures on exhibition. He sold one of his paintings to the late A. T. Stewart, of New York, for seventy thousand dollars, and probably has as high a reputation as any living artist. Most of his pictures are small ones, and the one, "The Philosopher," which is said to have the first award, reveals his power of rendering in detail every part of a painting to perfection. "The Review" is his largest painting, and is a brilliant scene of thousands of soldiers in their gay uniforms, bringing out in a life-like manner the spectacle of a grand military parade. His portrait of Alexandre Dumas is said to be admirable. From lack of proper education in art, no doubt, I could not understand why so great a value is put upon his works, and in my ignorance I should have selected two or three in the American Department as my choice. One, "Les Funérailles de une Momie," by Bridgman, was bought by James Gordon Bennett, of New York, for three thousand dollars, and to my mind is the choice of the United States paintings, among which I particularly noticed a tropical scene, by Church; "Playing a Violin by Candle-light," by Guy, and "The Passing Show," by J. G. Brown, portraying four street boys viewing the passing of one of Barnum's shows, in all their glee, pointing, gesticulating, etc., which is wonderfully life-like. Americans are fond of depreciating our display in art, but, considering the small number of paintings, there are as few poor ones among them as in the exhibit of any other nation. The French, of course, would undervalue them, as there are no nude pieces, of which there are numerous examples in the French Gallery which would shock the modesty of prudes, at least. You will see crowds of men and women enjoying or admiring one called "The Nymphs," where there are thirteen nymphs bathing and swinging and reposing themselves upon the velvety lawn under the shady trees; while in the thicket behind are two "Bohemians," peeping through the thick meshes of trees and vines.

I selected a painting in the French Gallery that I should like, by the distinguished artist Bouguereau. The subject is "Charity," representing a motherly, lovely woman, holding in her arms three orphan children, each clinging to her with intense earnestness, and looking into her face as if instinctively knowing that she loves them and would relieve them, reading aright her kindly and benevolent expression. At her feet a child on either side, nestling closely to her, one covering modestly its bare bosom with its arms, the other leaning on two volumes of the Bible and pointing its finger closely, as if spelling each syllable, toward the word " Evangelium," and under it the printed page which could not be read, but whose significance is apparent. By the side was gold coin spilled out from an iron safe, and in front a pile of gold, which was so well represented that it seemed as if you could take into your hand each piece. The figures were all so life-like and suggestive and characteristic that I thought what a beautiful illustration it was of the subject, and what a study for those who enjoy, portrayed upon canvas, anything which will elevate and refine the soul. Pictures upon the wall reveal the taste and character of the inmates of the home, and, if of the right kind, help to educate and refine us. What we see portrayed before us every day must have an effect upon the character. On making inquiry of Mr. E. F. Andrews, the artist from Columbus, and others, I learned that the painting I admired was one of the most valuable in the Exhibition, and could not be purchased for less than eight or ten thousand dollars.

As I walked through the galleries, looking at the paintings which attracted me most and trying to read the inscriptions — but not often with success — these paintings from so many different nations, speaking different tongues, nevertheless all breathe the same language; and it is a delight, after visiting the various departments of the Exhibition, to get away from the babel of speech and drink in inspiration from these mute representations of truth and beauty, as depicted by so many great and noble artists.

There are so many things here to attract admiration that a fuller description would occupy too much space, and perhaps fail to interest our readers. The Exposition is a grand success. The grounds and location of our own Centennial Exposition in 1876 were far more picturesque and beautiful, and the space occupied more than four times that of the Paris Exposition; and while the arrangement and unlimited expense laid out on the buildings of the latter make everything almost perfect, and while at the same time everything is compact and easily reached, yet it appears to me, all things considered, that we compared favorably with Paris, and that such an impression generally prevails. Paris, being so near the other old nations of the world, and her own productions making in themselves so grand a display, even if no other nation were represented, I cannot but feel, comparatively speaking, proud of our Centennial Exposition. To-day, but on a grander scale, the Exhibition of Paris recalls that of Philadelphia, by its general arrangement, by the classification of its contents and by the beauty of its exhibits. The price of admission is fixed at only one franc, or twenty cents, and great crowds of peasants, with blue cotton blouses, and their wives, with their short, cheap frocks and white caps, are to be seen enjoying the best things the world can produce. The number of exhibitors amounts to some sixty thousand, of whom about one-half are from France alone.

We meet here, as everywhere, a great many Americans, and do not find the prices for board at the hotels so high as we had been led to expect from letters and representations we had seen in newspapers at home. If one chooses to be imposed upon, it is very easy to go to the Grand Hotel and pay ten or fifteen dollars a day; but we found a good central location and as pleasant rooms as one could wish in the Boulevard Hausmann, at about three and a half dollars a day, including all meals. Our first meal is coffee and bread and butter, sent to our room at nine o'clock in the morning; breakfast, cold meat, etc., at twelve M.; dinner, *table d'hôte* (all dine at one table), at half-past six P. M.; and tea at half-past seven in the evening, which gives us a good long day for sight-seeing. The weather is cool and delightful here, and hence we are enabled to go about and accomplish a great deal of sight-seeing in a short time.

On Sunday we attended church at the American Chapel. On our way we could notice no difference in the appearance of the streets from that of any other day in the week. The workmen were busy as usual on the splendid stone buildings that are going up all over Paris. Stores were open, and on our return, coming down the Champs Élysées (the finest promenade in Europe), a panorama of the greatest gaiety presents itself. Upon each side are the numerous *cafés chantants*, for open-air concerts, which on summer evenings do not close until midnight. Bands of music were playing and crowds were gathering, for Sunday seems to be the grand holiday for Parisians. The central road is thronged with carriages and the side-ways with pedestrians. In the evening it was brilliantly illuminated, and one would think that the Sabbath was a grand fête day, like our national holiday, the Fourth of July. All the parks (and they are numerous in Paris) were crowded with people, and, with the fountains playing, presented an exciting scene.

XII.

FROM PARIS TO LUCERNE....LAKE OF THE FOUR FOREST CANTONS....ASCENT OF THE RIGI; SCENES AT SUNSET AND SUNRISE; THE RANZ DES VACHES....FLÜELEN.... HOME OF TELL....ST. GOTHARD PASS....GLACIER DU RHONE....THE HANSECK....SUNDAY AT INTERLAKEN.

Stresa, Italy.

FROM Paris our ride to Lucerne was mostly through a flat, uninteresting country, until we enter Switzerland at Mühlhausen, where we leave behind us "*Oui, oui, monsieur*," and hear instead "*Ja, ja, mein Herr.*" In the morning we get the first view of the Rhine at Basle, the greatest ribbon manufactory in Europe. It was at this place that we had our first experience with German feather-beds. It was a cold, uncomfortable night as we entered our rooms, whither we were shown by a tidy-looking servant-girl. Now, a German feather-bed is a peculiar institution—narrow, and so lofty that one needs a ladder to mount into it. As you trust yourself unwarily to its sleek-looking surface, you find yourself sinking into fathomless depths of feathers, and as you strive to enter and cover yourself for the night, you discover that you must slide yourself, sandwich fashion, between two immense sacks of down, whose heat and yielding softness, especially in summer, soon prove themselves unendurable. For my friend the Doctor, however, it was an experience altogether too trying; so he requested the chamber-maid, as well as he could, to bring him two woolen blankets. Off she ran, with the reply, "*Ja, ja, mein Herr,*" and soon returned with a glowing face and two additional feather-beds, one under each arm—making four in all for an August night. It was impossible for him to make her understand what he wanted. In France the Doctor had rather the advantage of me, insomuch as he spoke French, and I did not. But now came my turn: so, at the top of my voice, so that the girl might hear me in his room, I essayed to air my German, and shouted, "*Zwei wollene Bettdecken.*" With a merry laugh all round, the girl hurried off, and soon brought the blankets, and I had the satisfaction of knowing both that my German was understood and that the good Doctor was in no further danger of being smothered for the night.

All the way from Paris we notice peasants gathering their oats, wheat and hay, using the old-fashioned short scythe to cut their grain, and we only saw one mowing-machine in the whole distance of four hundred miles. As we pass, we observe whole families of men, women and children seated upon the grass, with their farm implements in their hands, resting themselves while the train passes, and looking in the distance like a picnic party. The morning ride was a delightful one, affording our first glimpse of the Bernese Oberland, and, riding along Lake Sesaporck, we also get our first view of a lake in Switzerland, and our attention is attracted by the quaint Swiss houses, their thatched roofs laid regularly with flat stones and their sides all covered over with small shingles, about one by two inches in size, and which, with their rounded ends, make them look like the scales of a fish. The word "Restauration," painted on numerous large buildings, indicated that here was a hotel or restaurant. We arrive at Lucerne, situated on the western extremity of the Lake of the Four Forest Cantons, or "Vierwaldstädter See," and our first walk through the town is to see the greatest curiosity of the place, a magnificent work of art by Thorwaldsen, wrought out of a lofty solid rock. It represents a dying lion, twenty-eight and one-half feet in length, transfixed by an arrow, and was designed to commemorate the Swiss Guards who died in defending the royal family of France in 1792. In front is a beautiful lake, with a fountain playing, and from the rock beside it a mountain stream leaps down. We cannot linger long, and after getting a view of the town and lake from the highest eminence, take the steamer on the lake for Vitznau, to ascend the Rigi.

The lake is said to be one of the most beautiful in the world, and from what we had read and heard from travelers we were prepared for unusual pleasure. Nothing could be more complete and satisfying than the grandeur of its mountain scenery, the quiet beauty of its banks, and the endless variety of its charms. Soon in the distance the Bernese Alps present themselves, with their summits covered

SUMMIT OF THE RIGI. VITZNAU.

with snow, and we see the two bays of Alpnach and Küssnacht stretching away to the west and east, and giving the lake the form of a cross. At Vitznau it seemed as though we had reached the end of the lake, for a promontory on the right and left somewhat overlap each other. We landed at the village of Vitznau, nestling in the little bay, to ascend the Rigi. "It would be like going to Rome and not seeing the Coliseum, or going to Naples and not seeing Pompeii," to come to Switzerland and not ascend the Rigi. We can either ascend on foot or take the railroad up the mountain three and a half miles. We prefer the latter, although we do not go over three miles an hour, "for every four feet of length the line rises one foot." The engine does not look like an ordinary locomotive, the boiler being upright, and when standing at the station it has an odd appearance. Every precaution is taken for safety, and the toothed wheel working between the rails, by which the train ascends, and the brakes by which the car can be held fast to the rack-rail, give us faith in the safety of the ascent. Up we go, across deep ravines and through tunnels, with splendid scenery all around us. The lake below and its surrounding views are charming to behold. We soon arrive at the summit, which towers up to the height of nearly six thousand feet; it is green with grass, and cows, sheep and goats are seen feeding in every direction.

We came to view the glorious scenes at sunset and at sunrise, but the prospect is gloomy enough. It is cold as winter; the rain pours down, and clouds cover the valleys and mountains. We go out, in our rubber overcoats, to catch every view possible. We watch a couple of hours, in hopes of obtaining a glimpse of old Sol as he takes his leave of us. We soon see his rays reflected upon the distant snow-covered Alps, and the gold and silver colored clouds, with a long line of greenish tint, encourage us to hope that we are to have a view to-night which many have been waiting a week to witness. We are not disappointed. Soon the clouds begin to lift, and form a dark, heavy bank. An immense ball of fire seems to drop slowly down, throwing its rays all over the horizon, and a scene of indescribable beauty presents itself. We hold within our vision a circumference of some three hundred miles—about one hundred and fifty miles of continuous snow-capped Alps on the east and south, with the grand old Jungfrau in the distance. The names of the different mountains are given us by our guide. Conspicuous stand the mountains of the Bernese Oberland. They present a magnificent appearance, with their mantles of eternal snow. Fourteen lakes are counted in full view. On the other side we see the towns of Lucerne, Zurich and many villages hugging the mountains by the banks of the lakes, and numerous Swiss chalets dotting the mountain sides. We linger until driven in-doors by the cold. I here undergo another experience in trying to sleep between two Dutch feather-beds, one above and one below, and, notwithstanding these adjuncts to warmth, I do not think that I ever suffered so much in one night from the cold. The feather-bed which was to cover me was sure to be where I could not find it, either on one side of me or on the floor; and as I looked around for a strap to fasten it over me without success, I was obliged to shiver with cold all night.

We were given warning that if we heard the Alpine horn—a wooden instrument some eight feet in length—at about half-past three o'clock in the morning, it would be an indication that the sun could be seen as it started on its journey from the east. We jump at the welcome sound, "Tra-da-tra-da-dui-da"; it is the "*Ranz des vaches,*" thrilling out into the fresh morning air, and, obeying its echoing notes, a motley crowd rush up the summit. A variety of strange costumes are to be seen; for men, women and children, fearful of missing the sunrise, make a hasty toilet or catch up a blanket or shawl. Brides and young ladies have evidently neglected the mirror, and, cold and shivering, pace to and fro the elevated height, waiting the appearance of the refulgent orb of day. The peaks of snow begin to change their colors, indifferently white at first, then yellowish, and at last turning to a lovely pink. One bright flash, and the first ray of the sun shoots forth. For a moment all is silent, then a shout goes up which makes the welkin ring, and the full splendor of the vast panorama is displayed. Presently a party of Americans, who were on the Belvedere, raised the stirring strains of "America," and a band of Swiss minstrels (making an Alpine walking tour), in their quaint costumes and knapsacks, sang "Praise to the Alps."

To me the evening view was more attractive than that of the morning. We were fortunate in being able to enjoy, on our first visit to the Rigi, views long to be remembered, and, well satisfied, take the steam-carriage down to Vitznau, and from there pursue our way by steamer up the lake to Flüelen, about twenty-five miles distant. The lake winds around among the mountains, and every little while one is surprised with a gallery of new and varied pictures. Of all lakes, either in California, the Eastern States, Ireland, Wales, England, Scotland or France, this is the most beautiful. Our own Lake George is next in picturesque and beautiful scenery. We take diligence at Flüelen through the Furca and St. Gothard passes, *via* Glacier du Rhone, etc., to Interlaken. We pass, between Flüelen and Altorf, Theodore Tilton (looking as serene as a thunder-cloud) and his two daughters, walking. They evidently came down the lake, and were on their way to Altorf to see a colossal statue of William Tell, marking the spot where the Swiss hero stood when he aimed at the apple on his son's head. Altorf is near Bürglen, the birthplace and home of Tell, where is also a chapel, painted over with scenes from his life, and supposed to mark the site of his house.

We begin to realize that we are in the land of Tell, as so many of the hotels, restaurants and pensions (boarding-houses) are called by his name. After crossing the Schächenbach ("in the waters of which Tell perished while struggling to save a child"), the ascent of St. Gothard is soon begun. It is not over a single peak or eminence, but over a mountainous group, presenting a wild and magnificent appearance, winding around among the mountains by the River Reuss, which here dashes madly along, foaming and leaping over its rocky bed. Numerous water-falls come plunging down the declivities, and the ride to Andermatt is a grand one. We pass the Devil's Bridge and many places of historic interest, occasioned by the deadly struggles in the wars between France, Germany and Russia in 1799.

The Alps are ranged about a central spot west of the St. Gothard Pass, where about a hundred square miles of rock, etc., lie above the limits of perpetual snow, while the Galenstock and other mountains rise to the height of from ten to twelve thousand feet. "The waters of this elevated region pass by the Rhine to the German Ocean, by the Rhone to the Mediterranean, by the Po to the Adriatic, and by the Danube to the Black Sea." At Andermatt we encountered a snow-storm. It is the chief village of the valley. A tunnel is being cut through the mountain, which is to be nine and a half miles long, and is to be called the St. Gothard Tunnel, a wonderful work of engineering. It will be the longest one in the world. Workmen by the thousand are engaged upon it, and it is to be finished in 1880. They have already been at work upon it six or eight years. We found a good hotel at Andermatt, and although their summer is so short for the raising of produce, being only four months in duration, they gave us a better dinner, and served in better style, than any that we have had since coming to Europe, and all for four francs, or eighty cents. There were eight different courses, with plates removed each time. The courses after soup were as follows: fish, roast beef, boiled tongue with greens, chicken with salad, plum pudding, cake, and, lastly, fruit and nuts. I spent another cold night under a feather-bed, and concluded I must try something else to keep me warm, if I am to remain long in this region of ice and snow.

Our passage from here, by private conveyance and our own good walkers, brought us to the Glacier du Rhone, where we first hear the sound of an avalanche, like distant thunder. Our guide had spent six years in America, and could therefore talk English enough to point out to us all the objects of interest—the different mountains and glaciers. We pass the Tiefer glacier on the northern flank, and the Siedeln glacier on the southern. Hepworth Dixon, in "The Switzers," says: "Three years ago a cave was entered by this Tiefer glacier, and then the noblest crystals in the world were found. The rock was topaz. Fragments lay about in heaps, each broken piece a hundred or two hundred pounds in weight. Some fifteen tons of topaz were removed from this great hiding-place of Nature in a single year. What sage can count the mounds yet lurking near this 'Pillar of the Sun'?" The descent from the Furca Pass is by a series of zigzags, very abrupt, and giving the unnecessarily nervous traveler the impression that he is going to the bottom with a bound. The Rhone glacier—that great sea of ice extending for fifteen miles—is passed, resembling the American water-fall at Niagara if frozen up. I walked over this consolidated mass and entered a natural grotto of ice, winding under the glacier, about eight feet high and from one to two hundred feet long. I thought that if this mass of ice were in Paris (ice beneath us, ice above us, ice all about us), we should not have to pay twenty cents a week extra for it at our hotel there, as we did.

We make the ascent of the Hanseck, seven thousand one hundred and three feet in height, and traverse numerous snow-drifts firm enough to bear up a horse, and pass the Todtensee. Here, in 1799, French and Austrians closed in deadly struggle, and the dead were buried in the lake. One would naturally suppose that these mountains would be a barrier to war. We were glad to get to the Grimsel Hospice to rest for the night. This hospice was formerly a monastic refuge down among the little lakes, with snow-capped mountains and water-falls all around. We were shown a new part to the house, where an avalanche came down last year and took off a corner. It rained all night, and in the morning it was dismal enough; but the idea of spending the Sabbath here, among the noisy guides, when we had expected to be at Interlaken, was altogether too much for us. We therefore thought it a good time to test our rubber overcoats and Western pluck, and, although warned that the day would be a stormy one, took the bridle-path to Meyringen, over what is called a seven-hour walk. As we wound our way across the mountains, by the roaring River Aar, crossing it many times, with the cataracts thundering down the steep declivities, the rain beating upon us and the wind whistling about our ears, I said to the Doctor: "What is the romance in crossing the Alps and not braving a storm?" "Oh, yes," he replied, "make a virtue of necessity." We stopped at the only chalet on the path to Imhof and dried our clothes, and then visited the Handeck Falls, the finest in Switzerland, where the Aar leaps down two hundred and fifty feet at a bound, to which, half way down, the Erlenbach, entering at right angles, joins its falling waters. Agassiz here studied glacial action, and left his name carved on the rock of a mountain named after him, which the guide pointed out to us. His experiments on glacial action proved that one of these glaciers moves at the rate of eight inches a day, or eighty-five yards a year. We were glad to roam about so lovely a spot as Meyringen, where we visit the falls of the Alpach and of the Reichenbach. We stopped at an excellent hotel, and, finding that the rain had penetrated our rubber overcoats, stripped off our wet clothes to dry them, and then took diligence for Brienz, and from there by Lake Brienz to Interlaken. This lake is nearly surrounded by mountains, and it was delightful to glide again over placid waters, quite in contrast with the roughness of our day's experiences. The clouds had cleared away, and we rode on to the Giessbach Falls. Here many passengers left us to pass the Sabbath. These falls are illuminated with Bengola lights, for the benefit of visitors, every evening.

Sunday at Interlaken is delightful, for it is a charming place. Our hotel fronts the Jungfrau, whence one of the finest views in Switzerland is obtained. The mountain this morning was covered with snow, and the white, fleecy clouds, lower down, lay in folds as beautiful as those of a rich, white satin dress. We were tolled to the Scotch Presbyterian Church, and heard an excellent sermon from Rev. Dr. White, of Edinburgh, which was full of rest and refreshment after the week's pleasuring among the grand scenery of the Alps. I think that mountains such as are found in California and Switzerland, full of sublime scenery, are an expression of God's benediction,—"A pure speaking to the spirit of man of that power and love upon which the soul may rest as upon the everlasting rock." I do not believe it is wise for us to read the vengeance of God in the mountain crag, the lightning flash and the ocean storm. Does not such a theology as has been preached—that God's wrath is depicted in the mountains, the thunder and the fury of the tempest, as indicative of His power and justice—drive us rather to fear than to love Him?

Interlaken is situated between two lakes (as its name implies), about two miles apart. It is supposed that these were formerly one body of water, but were divided by the earth deposits from the mountain streams into the two present basins. The dividing belt is from one-half to a mile broad, and about two miles long. From here numerous excursions can be made up the mountains, and the one that we chose for our day's delectation was by the bridle-path up the Schynige Platte, six thousand one hundred and eighty feet high. We were delighted with the views of the valleys and lakes—Thun and Brienz, and the Snow Mountains—which seem just across the narrow valley from us, glittering in the sunshine like Peruvian silver, and appearing to belong more to heaven than to earth.

XIII.

DESCRIPTION OF THE SWISS CAPITAL....GENEVA AND ITS HISTORIC ASSOCIATIONS....LOVELY LAKE LEMAN.... THE VALE OF CHAMOUNI....MER DE GLACE....OVER THE SIMPLON PASS....FAREWELL TO SWITZERLAND.

Stresa, Italy.

WE leave beautiful Interlaken with regret, passing down Lake Thun for Berne. On both sides of the lake are rustic villages, and hill-sides dotted here and there with chalets, villas and gardens, backed by the snowy giants of the Oberland.

Berne is the capital of the Swiss Confederacy, and one of the most ancient cities in Europe. It was market-day when we arrived, and a good opportunity was thus afforded of seeing the peasantry and market people, with their quaint costumes and odd style of vehicles. Here the houses are so constructed as to form an arcade over the foot-ways, through which we traversed the city. This, in cold, snowy weather, or rainy (as it is to-day), has its advantages; but, as we walked through the Regent Street Quadrant, the stores looked dark and gloomy, while all the goods seemed to be exposed outside the shops, and as we pass along we notice the trading going on with the different customers outside. The old clock-tower is a noticeable feature. "Whenever the clock strikes, at three minutes before the hour, a cock crows and flaps his wings; presently some bears march in procession round an old man, and the cock crows again. Then a fool strikes the hour on a bell with a hammer, while the old man checks off the strokes with his scepter, and turns his hour-glass. A bear nods approval, and a final bout of cock-crowing ends the performance."

A rich agricultural district lies between Berne and Lausanne, and at this latter place we obtain our first view of Lake Geneva, along whose lovely banks the remainder of our route by rail passes to the city of the same name. The view of the lake and the glimpse of the distant mountains from our window in the Hotel National, in the morning, are very striking. Geneva is the largest city in Switzerland, and is about the size of Columbus. Our ride through the city this cool, delightful morning will not soon be forgotten, nor the many places of interest we visited — among others the Cathedral in which Calvin preached, where we stood beneath the canopy of the pulpit which he occupied and sat in his chair, and afterward visited the house where he lived for nineteen years, and where, in 1564, he died. Near by is the Hotel de Ville (City Hall), the tower of which was built in the fifteenth century. In order to enter the council chamber we ascend a paved inclined plane, used instead of a staircase, to the height of four or five stories, and which the old Councilmen themselves, in former times, used to enter on horseback.

The place of most interest to us in this building was the small chamber, about twenty-two feet by thirty, where sat the Arbitration Commissioners on the Alabama Claims, in 1872. There are only two windows in the room, opening out upon a bushy garden. On the right, as you enter, you notice a handsome white marble tablet in commemoration of the American Commission, dated Geneva, 14th September, 1872, etc., etc. Inscribed in French on the other side is a like tablet in commemoration of some Swiss Commission. As we leave the apartment we notice on the right photographs of the American Commissioners and their ladies, prominent among whom are Chief Justice Waite and Hon. Charles Francis Adams, with their wives. On the other side are the English Commissioners. Not far away is the Academie, a beautiful stone building. It contains the Bibliotheque Publique and a great number of manuscripts, among which are autograph letters of Calvin, Luther, Melancthon, etc. There are also a great number of portraits. We asked for one of Servetus, the Spanish Unitarian condemned to be burned by Calvin. The guide shook his head, but presently brought it to us, after several times being requested to do so. I watched him as he returned it to its hidden place in one corner of the library. The label under it is in French, which, translated, runs, " Burnt in Geneva, to the honor and glory of God." We inquired of the guide as to the spot where Servetus was burned, and he pointed to the window and replied in French, "The place is all covered over with buildings."

Geneva is a quiet, beautiful spot—the most

attractive place in which to pass a few months of leisure of any we have seen in Switzerland. The environs, commanding views of Mont Blanc and the distant mountains, are all that one could wish. The Lake of Geneva (Lake Lemanus of the Romans) is in the shape of a crescent, and so much has been written, sung and preached in its praise that almost every one seems to have some acquaintance with it. As we take a delightful ride, viewing the beautiful villages and cultivated fields upon its banks, we notice that the color of the water is blue, while that of the other Swiss lakes is green. Byron has written more than any other poet about Lake Leman, and many will call to mind the lines:

> "Lake Leman wooes me with its crystal face,
> The mirror where the stars and mountains view
> The stillness of their aspect in each trace
> Its clear depth yields of their fair height and hue."

Our all-day ride by coach and six (or rather diligence) to Chamouni, with its varied scenery, and in full view of Mont Blanc, was simply charming. On our arrival, the clouds lifted from the mountains, around which they had clung for a week, showing

Mont Blanc in all his glory, towering up to an altitude of fifteen thousand seven hundred and eighty-one feet. Standing in the little vale of Chamouni, right under this monarch of hills, at the foot of the Glacier du Bossons, we witnessed the setting sun reflecting his splendors upon the snow. It was an awe-inspiring scene, only equaled by our first sight, from Inspiration Point, of the Yosemite Valley, in California. The Yosemite Valley, however, is much longer and wider and grander than the valley of Chamouni, and there is no scenery in Switzerland or the world to compare with it, remembering, as one does, its towering walls of granite, its numerous water-falls, and the stream of the Yosemite itself plunging precipitously down two thousand five hundred feet. We must ascend Montanvert, six thousand three hundred and two feet high, and see the Mer de Glace (sea of ice), and so we rise early, and with our guide *and fifty other goats*, each of the latter with a bell, however, start at six A. M. on our tramp. The goats, going to their mountain pastures, soon outstrip us in the race, as they run up the steep rocks, while we wind round and round to seek an easier ascent.

We cross the Mer de Glace with great difficulty—the ice is so slippery and such immense crevasses meet us. We look into one worn by the running water to a depth of three hundred feet, and stick our alpenstocks hard into the ice, not wishing to descend into the depths of this frightful well. Around us on every side are mountains of snow, with Mont Blanc towering above them all. We descended by the "*Mauvais Pas*," cut in the side of the cliffs, and although at one place we would gladly have stopped to admire the scene, our guide hurried us on, for we heard the sound of crashing rocks, and, looking up, saw how little apparently kept them from coming down upon us. We catch the echo of the avalanche in the distance, and quicken our pace. At length we approach the glacier. Far down in the valley stands a little clump of Swiss cottages, looking as if at any moment they might be swept away by the snow and ice. Our ride lies across the Tête Noire, to Martigny, about nine hours distant, passing several glaciers and down by little villages, where we notice numerous walls to ward off the fall of the avalanches. Here the women are the burden-bearers, and we meet them in the narrow paths with

great loads of hay, covering their entire bodies save their lower limbs. This hay they are conveying from their little meadow-patches, where it is prepared for the barn, situated usually underneath their houses, and whence the debris from their stables is thrown out and heaped up directly under their windows. Everywhere we encounter them in the winding paths, laden like pack-mules with their grassy burdens, and are sometimes obliged to back out in order to pass them, and occasionally we even come into lively collision with each other—incidents which add to the interest of the day.

A night's rest at Martigny, before starting over the Simplon Pass into Italy, was very acceptable. The road we take across the Alps was constructed by Napoleon after the famous battle of Marengo, and our ride to-day of twenty-two hours, to Stresa, on Lago Maggiore, culminated in the most magnificent scenery which we had looked upon in our two weeks of enchanting Swiss travel. This grand panorama of the Alps cannot be described; its real grandeur is beyond the power of words to paint, but its varied scenes will long be vividly impressed upon our memory. On the summit of the pass, six thousand six hundred feet high, is the Hospice, managed by Augustine monks, an immense building standing out alone and capable of entertaining three hundred souls. No charge is made for entertainment, but all are expected to give something toward the support of the Catholic Church. We are glad to be on the descent once more; we pass through gigantic tunnels hewn out of solid rock, with the water from the glaciers rushing down over and under the roadway, and even trickling in through the lookouts in the tunnel — the rushing torrents affording us views of a wondrous variety of water-falls. I thought the most sublime sight of a deep gorge that I ever saw was the Arkansas Cañon, in Colorado; but our ride this afternoon along the boiling waters of the Fressinone, where the rocks rise almost perpendicularly more than two thousand feet, and the roadway is hewn out of the solid wall, was certainly a grander view.

We have now been about two weeks in Switzerland, among its mountains of snow and ice, its beautiful lakes and shifting glaciers, and the change from a bracing atmosphere, where we needed our warmest winter clothing and overcoats, to the warm sunshine and balmy air of Italy, is indeed remarkable. We come suddenly upon the beautiful Lake Maggiore, with charming islands studding its bosom, and stop to rest for the Sabbath at the lovely village of Stresa, surrounded by fine scenery both of land and water, and here obtain our first realizing view of sunny Italy.

Switzerland is certainly a wonderful country, and to Swiss scenery I have but vainly tried to do justice. Its impression is amazing, and is beyond the reach even of the poet to adequately express. "Nature-like, her own atmospheric influences come upon the imagination with imperceptible but overpowering force, and will not let herself be scanned and her features accurately described. She is very lofty, pure and divine, hiding herself from the gaze of man, and with depths of meaning that are no more to be fathomed than the divine source from which they sprang."

XIV.

Sunny Italy.... Lago Maggiore and the Borromean Islands.... Milan and its Cathedral.... The City of Palaces.... Monument to Columbus.... Pisa: the Campo Santo, Duomo and Leaning Tower.... Rome: Festival of the Assumption of the Virgin: St. Peter's, The Vatican, and their Art Treasures.

Rome, Italy.

WE spent a delightful Sabbath at Lake Maggiore, the largest of all the Italian lakes that lie embosomed in the beautiful scenery at the foot of the Alps. The most charming view of the Lake is from the little village of Stresa, with the Borromean Islands in full sight. The sail around them by moonlight, with the peculiar, mellow Italian sky bounding the horizon, the placid waters of the lake, the Alps in distant view, and the numerous houses upon the islands gay with lights, together with the sweet sound of evening bells, and nought else to break the silence but the keel of the boat as it divides the rippling waves, afforded an hour of pleasure which we will never forget. Departing from the splendid hotel, we gaze back regretfully upon the unequaled scenery of the spot. There was Church of England service, with preaching, in the parlors of the hotel. The rector prayed for the Queen of England, the Prince of Wales, the royal family and all in authority in England, the King of Italy, and for the President of the United States. The latter was feebly responded to; but one was present from Ohio who rang out the response so earnestly as unintentionally to attract observation. My first sight of the Italian people was at the Cathedral, where I attended service on Sunday afternoon, and heard a sermon in Italian from the priest. The congregation, composed mostly of women and children, seemed to be from the poorer class of people. Not a woman or girl present had on a bonnet, but they wore instead bright-colored shawls drawn closely over their heads, and when out of doors, in the hot sun, many went with their heads uncovered. Our passage down the lake and by railroad, giving us a magnificent view of the Alps from Somma (where a battle between Scipio and Hannibal took place, B. C. 218), and on to Milan, was uninteresting. Here we are introduced to Italian life. The great attraction of Milan is the grand old Cathedral, the Duomo, the largest Gothic edifice in the world. On entering, one's sight is greeted with a forest of pillars, fifty-two in number, extending in four rows the whole length of the building—four hundred and seventy-seven feet. As you walk up and down between these magnificent columns you begin to realize something of the size of the building and the beauty of its proportions. Immediately within the nave, a meridian line has been laid down across the mosaic pavement of red, white and blue marble. This the sun's rays cross at mid-day. The church itself is built of white marble, and a part was shown us which was but just finished. We ascended to the roof and tower. There is a central tower and spire, and the building literally bristles with pinnacles, which give it an indescribably light and airy effect, in spite of its immense size. There are six thousand marble statues adorning its exterior, and there is room for

MILAN CATHEDRAL.

fifteen thousand more. A new one is added every little while, to the number, perhaps, of from fifteen to twenty a year. Some of them are of great merit, and it is said that for one, " Rebecca," the Empress of Russia, noticing it as she passed, offered twenty-five thousand francs, or five thousand dollars. Not a statue is allowed to be put in position unless it has merit. One part of the ornamentation upon the roof, a view of which we obtain from the tower, is called the "Flower Garden," on account of its numerous floral decorations in marble. The present cathedral was begun in 1386. It is very nearly the size of St. Paul's, in London, and, with the exception of the grand cathedral at Seville, may be considered next in dimensions to St. Peter's at Rome. The view from the tower is the finest to be had from any church tower in the world—to the north and west the Alps, to the east the line of the Mediterranean, and to the west the Adriatic Sea. The battle-field of Magenta and the scenes of various other historic conflicts are visible. There are eighty churches in Milan, among which we visited that of St. Ambrose, dating from the twelfth century. A Catholic priest showed us the iron gates shut by the

Archbishop against the Emperor Theodosius until he had made repentance for the destruction of some five or six thousand men for some trivial cause.

As we walked up and down the beautiful covered arcade, the largest in the world, where the principal retail trade is carried on, we noticed the splendidly dressed, dark-complexioned, black-eyed Italian ladies, with only black veils on their heads, which depended gracefully behind. Not one, I think, had on a hat or bonnet. Most of their dresses seemed to be of black material, and some were elegantly trimmed with red. On the streets, many of the women that we saw were without any coverings to their heads in the hot sun, though some carried parasols.

Our ride to Genoa, the "City of Palaces," was through a level region until we entered the Apennine district. Genoa is of about the same size as Milan — over two hundred thousand population — but quite in contrast as to situation. About Milan it is flat and level as about Columbus; while Genoa, in the inequalities of its situation, is one of the finest and loveliest places in the world. It is a "splendid amphitheater, terrace rising above terrace, garden upon garden, palace upon palace, height upon height."

The first bank in the world of which we have any record, the "Bank of St. George," was in existence here before Columbus crossed the Atlantic, and was making loans and receiving deposits at that time. The building is now occupied as the Custom House. Genoa has erected a splendid monument in honor of Columbus, who was born near by, at Cogoleto. It is of white marble, surmounted by a splendid statue of the great discoverer, which rests upon an anchor, with the kneeling figure of America at his feet. Around are the allegorical figures of Religion, Wisdom, Force and Geography, in a sitting posture, between which are reliefs representing the scenes in his history. In the little park surrounding the whole, the plants—pampas grass, colodiums, callas, etc.—seemed singularly appropriate, and made us think of home. Genoa is one of the most flourishing, growing cities we have seen. Numerous fine buildings and various improvements are in progress, and it has one of the best war harbors in the world.

The ride by rail to Pisa, along the Mediterranean, was sufficiently varied. We passed, I should think, through at least ten tunnels; we rushed through promontories; rounded a beautiful bay; and then, through the marble mountains, dashed past the world-famous quarries of Carrara, and came at length to Pisa, where we get our first view of the Arno. The romance is all taken out of the "beautiful" Arno when we see what a turbid stream it is. We pass the Campo Santo (cemetery), where fifty-three shiploads of holy ground from Palestine were brought by Archbishop Ubaldo, in A. D. 1200, that in it the devout might find burial. Here stands one of the wonders of the world, the Leaning Tower. It is one hundred and fifty-one feet in height and twelve feet out of perpendicular, and, as you look up from the base on the side that overhangs your head, you are inclined to get out of the way, not caring to be crushed, although it has been in that position for over seven hundred years. This was a fête day, and the splendid cathedral was filled with people. This edifice is considered remarkably perfect architecturally. Its interior contains, among other interesting objects, the celebrated bronze lamp, hanging in the nave, which is said to have first suggested to Galileo the idea of the pendulum. The Cathedral, together with the Baptistery and Leaning Tower, is in an open part of the city; and being in close vicinity to each other, they form in themselves an imposing and unrivaled group. They are constructed of white and colored marbles, and their style of architecture is grand and impressive. Pisa was once a flourishing city, but now looks old and dilapidated. The house is shown in which Galileo was born, opposite the beautiful little chapel of San Andrea. Over the door is a white marble slab: "Here was born Galileo Galilei, February 15, 1564." Here, as in all Italian cities, are numerous old churches and other places of interest; but of these a passing traveler can only select a few of the most notable for description. Scarcely a foot of Italian soil is other than a pilgrimage.

The country between Pisa and Rome, for over two hundred miles, is desolate enough, with scarcely a habitation below Civita Vecchia. As we enter Rome, the end and goal of our travel is reached, and we begin to see at once those relics of antiquity dating back more than two thousand years, and which possess so vast and varied a history from the time of Romulus to the present. As we enter the city we catch a glimpse of the ruins of the Temple of Minerva Medica, and a part of the ancient wall of Servius Tullius, built 578 B. C. Everywhere, as we ride through the old city, we are reminded by the ruins that we are in Rome, and realize why pilgrims flock to it to-day as they have hitherward flocked for nearly two thousand years. It was formerly considered imprudent to visit Rome in July and August, but now it is as clean as any city we have passed through, and old residents consider it as healthy in these months as any other Italian city. The weather is no hotter here than in Columbus. The thermometer stands, out of doors, in the middle of the day, at from eighty to ninety degrees, and in-doors at seventy. The evenings and nights are delightful, and a cool breeze meets us as we ride about the city. We rest during the middle of the day, but clothe ourselves in our warm, woolen flannels to avoid the deadly chill as we enter the old Catacombs under ground, and also the cool atmosphere in the thick-walled churches, where the heat and light of the sun do not penetrate. One cannot be too careful in regard to atmospheric changes when traveling abroad.

It was during our stay here that the grand annual

festival of the "Assumption of the Virgin" was held, on August 15, in the Basilica of Sta. Maria Maggiore, which is the oldest church edifice in the city, founded A. D. 352. Business places are closed, and it seems everywhere like Sunday, for the people are all out for a holiday. The services in the church are grand and imposing. We were especially delighted with the music at vespers, which always calls forth a great crowd of the best people, and, indeed, all classes go with their families to hear this music, for which great preparation had been going on for months. The voices of about fifty male singers poured forth glorious and harmonious strains, such as one may often hear at any of our great concerts. The soprano was especially fine, and attracted much attention. We looked around for a female singer, but on inquiry were told, "No ladies can perform here; the voice comes from a eunuch." We had an opportunity of seeing the Italians in their holiday attire, and the better class of ladies appeared in their fashionable dresses, just as ours do in America; but the poorer classes looked dowdy, and many of them wore bodices, in bright colors, different in material from the skirt. The Pope usually comes out on the balcony and gives the benediction from there. During this festival high mass is performed in his presence; but since Victor Emmanuel became king of Italy and took up his residence in Rome, the late Pope considered himself a prisoner, and kept himself shut up in the Vatican. The present Pope does the same, and therefore much of the attractiveness of these holidays has passed away, and Rome is not what it used to be in the days of the temporal supremacy of the church.

There was a large number of cardinals and priests in the chapel where the music was performed. They occupied two rows of seats, arranged like those of an amphitheater, around the choir, and were dressed in all their splendor of gold, black, white and crimson robes. Those in black and crimson had a kind of white lace cape thrown over their shoulders. They were all old men and had splendid heads. The young ecclesiastics present looked as earnest, devout and intelligent as any of our theological students in Princeton or Andover. We notice confessions going on, and the old priest would take a rod occasionally and rap the woman confessing, as though something were wrong, and the penitent would depart, I suppose with full absolution granted. It was interesting to notice confessionals with signs over them for the Italians, the French, the Spaniards, the Germans, the English, etc. The good Lord understands all languages, and no doubt will forgive them their short-comings if they are sincere, even though forgiveness be asked through a priest.

We have seen so much here that one is at a loss to know where to begin and where to leave off, when all that may be said of the Eternal City must be confined within the moderate bounds of an ordinary chapter. Our first visit was naturally to St. Peter's, the largest church edifice in the world, built on the site where once stood a temple of Jupiter. "There has only been a change in spelling—Jupiter having merely given way to Jew-Peter." Our approach to the church, after first gazing at the wonderful dome and trying to realize its beauty, was through the immense colonnades which sweep around on either side of the great piazza. These colonnades contain each one hundred and forty-two columns, forty-two feet high, and inclose an area, elliptical in shape, of nearly eight hundred feet, through which the Pope and cardinals march or drive when they go in procession to the church. These immense colonnades have a grand and imposing appearance, and prepare one for the awe-inspiring building which he is about to enter, through the great pillars of the portico, whose dimensions are two hundred and thirty-five feet in length, forty-two in width and sixty-six in height. When you enter you are at first disappointed, and not until you walk the whole length of the building, six hundred and thirteen feet, and view the dome, transept, nave and grand arches, and the immense space between the pillars, do you begin to comprehend that you are in the largest and most splendid building in the world. We walked about and tried many times to realize where we were, and found that each time enlarged our mental capacity, so that our ideas began to expand sufficiently to get a full and overpowering conception of the magnitude and glory of St. Peter's. Some one has made a calculation that "a dozen churches of the size of Trinity Church of New York could be set within it, the fronts and steeples grouped around in a close circle, and there would be abundant room, while the top of the cluster of spires would not reach within an hundred feet of the inside of the dome." If the buildings on Broad street, from High street to the Irving House, north to Gay street and west to High street and south to Broad street, were cleared away, there would be about room enough for St. Peter's Church, and to include the Vatican you would have to go as far east as the Cathedral.

The Vatican, in which the Pope and seventy-two cardinals reside, is entered from the end of the right colonnade of the piazza of St. Peter's, and contains four thousand four hundred and twenty-two rooms. It covers a space of one thousand one hundred and fifty-one feet in length by seven hundred and sixty-seven in breadth, so the Pope's prison is a large one, and he has plenty of room to receive his friends, and enough paintings, etc., to cultivate his æsthetic tastes. The day on which we visited the Vatican was his reception day, and a great crowd were seeking admission, mostly ladies, handsomely dressed, with the black lace veil hanging over their heads, and falling over their shoulders to the ground. They seemed very happy and chatty, and many of them were handsome brunettes. We went first to the Sistine Chapel, where are the frescoes of Michael Angelo, which make it one of the art treasuries of the world. His "Last Judgment" is at the end of the chapel. The flat central portion of the ceiling contains nine pictures, the arched sides of the ceiling twelve. All the other frescoes in this room are by masters of the fifteenth century. Three rooms in the Vatican were decorated by Raphael, and they are considered among his chief productions in fresco. The "Disputa" is said to be one of his finest. We examined all the pictures by Raphael, Murillo and others among the noblest artists that the world has produced, seeking so to cultivate our tastes and feelings that we might truly enjoy these precious works. In one room are only three pictures; of these the "Transfiguration," by Raphael, which was unfinished at the time of his death, and is considered his masterpiece, is the most attractive and the oftenest copied. The works of art in the Vatican form a collection unparalleled in extent, interest and value, and it would take months to thoroughly examine them.

XV.

Reminiscences of Rome....The Coliseum....Ancient Baths and Catacombs....The Quirinal.....Bay and City of Naples....Ascent of Vesuvius....Pompeii and its Wonders....Off for New Scenes.

Rome, Italy.

TAKING a carriage, we ride over the Appian Way toward Albano, passing numerous old ruins of palaces, arches, tombs, churches, catacombs, etc., dating back two thousand years. The Campagna of Rome is a pure source of unfailing delight. St. Paul came into Rome a prisoner for trial, and the place is shown us where he was met by his friends from the city, and he "thanked God and took courage." We see in the distance the Sabine Mountains, calling to mind that old tale of history, that the Romans, over two thousand years ago, became wife-hungry, and carried off the Sabine women to fill the wifely office. The names of Cæsar, Cicero, etc., who took a prominent part in the world in their day, and who walked these streets and inhabited these now crumbling ruins, recall that which seemed to me almost a fable, when, as a boy, I read Cicero's masterly orations in his native tongue, and Virgil and Sallust; and now I am among the scenes narrated. We visit the old Mamertine Prison. It is said that St. Peter and St. Paul were imprisoned here, and a hole in the staircase in the wall is shown us, protected by iron bars, said to be the impression of St. Peter's head, when pushed against it by the jailer.

The Coliseum is, perhaps, one of the most interesting of ancient amphitheaters, and fills every pilgrim with wonder at its vast proportions. It is in the form of an ellipse and more than a third of a mile in circumference; it accommodated nearly one hundred thousand spectators, and must have been one of the grandest works of architecture that ever existed. Here thousands of the earlier Christians suffered martyrdom, by being thrown into the arena to be torn and devoured by savage beasts, while the thousands of spectators cheered and shouted with delight. The pens for the wild animals that were used in these gladiatorial exhibitions are still to be seen, together with many other local antiquarian discoveries.

We pass an obelisk brought from Egypt, where it was erected seventeen hundred years before Christ. In the Church of St. John Lateran they show us the tabernacle said to contain the heads of St. Peter and St. Paul. We enter the portico containing the Scala Santa, or Holy Staircase, said to have been ascended by our Saviour on his way to the Judgment Hall of Pilate. The staircase can only be mounted on one's knees. It was whilst Luther was making the ascent of the Scala Santa that he remembered the text, "The just shall live by faith," and, arising from his knees, he abruptly left the place, and from that time commenced his grand work and labor in the great Reformation which shook the world with its influence and power. The Baths of Caracalla were opened A. D. 216, and extended over an area which measured a quarter of a mile each way. The wonderful luxury of the ancient Romans, as depicted in all these ruins, is nowhere more vividly exemplified than here, where magnificent baths were erected, computed to have been sufficiently large to accommodate sixteen hundred persons at the same time, together with their adjuncts of libraries and lecture-rooms under the same roof. Besides these, there were seven other baths in imperial Rome of the same description. We descended into the Catacombs, where are the tombs of the early Christians and the places where they assembled for worship, for fear of being murdered by the pagans if their meetings should be discovered. The whole road called the Appian Way seemed to be lined with sepulchers, so that one here gets a good idea of the immense tombs which border the various other highways out of the city. Indeed, I have been so much about and among these old ruins that I begin to fear that, unless I stop and see something else, I myself shall turn into a mummy. The Quirinal Hill is one of the most beautiful parts of Rome, and from it we obtain a splendid view of the city. The palace of the same name is occupied by the King and Queen of Italy. This building also contains an immense number of paintings. Indeed, one could spend months in examining the various works of art, both in private and public collections, as well as the antiquities which abound in Rome and its environs. The Pantheon, near the corner of the principal street of the city—founded B. C. 27—is the best preserved of any of its ancient edifices, and in it rest the bodies of Raphael, the prince of painters, and Victor Emmanuel, the first king of United Italy. The portico of this old temple (which is greatly admired) is one hundred and ten feet long and forty-four wide, and is supported on sixteen columns. The interior is one hundred and forty-three feet in diameter, and the dome has the peculiarity of being open at the top, and the effect of the passing clouds, as one gazes up from the pavement below, is both unique and interesting.

We enter the Church of St. Paul, on the traditional site of the Apostle's execution. It incloses three fountains, which are said to have broken forth in the spots where the decapitated head of St. Paul three times touched the ground. The Basilica of St. Paul, which was burned in 1823, is more modern than the other churches, and is remarkable for its floors, columns, altars, etc., of the most splendid marble in Italy. Of these there are about seven kinds in the floor alone, polished like glass and most beautiful and refreshing to the eye after rambling among the mosaics and marble floors and columns of two thousand years ago.

But how can we leave Italy without seeing Naples, Vesuvius, Pompeii and Herculaneum? So we take the cars on a beautiful night, with the mellow light of the moon falling on these ancient ruins as we hurry by, giving them a peculiar, monumental look of the past, and in the morning arrive at Naples in time to wander through the streets, where we see all around us a city reminding us more of the towns of modern Egypt than of Europe. The asses, with immense loads of semi-tropical fruits, covering them all except their legs and ears with the heaped-up baskets; the swarthy men, more like Arabs than like Europeans; the great loads of men, women and children, piled swarming into a two-horse vehicle like a cart; together with the uproar and confusion of the streets, made me think of the descriptions that we hear of Cairo or of Alexandria. We drive for miles along the beautiful shores, and stop at the *"Hotel Royal des Etrangers,"* with a splendid outlook upon the bay, and Vesuvius on fire in the distance.

Ascent of Vesuvius.

Along this lovely bay we must go at once, twelve miles by train to Pompeii, and make our arrangements to ascend Vesuvius. We have some trouble in getting started on horseback. The guides want extra pay after the bargain is concluded. Italians are notorious for their duplicity, and you must have everything positive and well understood between you and them before you start, or trouble will come on settlement. As I mounted my horse half a dozen beggars jumped as if they would hold him, put my foot in the stirrup, etc., and all wanted pay. Finally we got started. I found two guides had laid hold of my horse's tail and were urging him forward at a break-neck speed. I let him go, and they managed to keep up with him, running as fast as he in the hot sun, giving me thus some idea of the speed with which the Arabians run beside their horses in the desert. We pass fig-orchards and immense vineyards, for grapes flourish clear up to the very foot of Vesuvius. Beggars annoy us at every village, and we notice that women are out of doors and in the fields with nothing on their heads, and that men and women and children are lying by the roadside resting in the broiling sun. The houses all have flat roofs, and their inmates sit out upon them, doing there also their washing and other work, thus giving everything quite an Oriental appearance. After riding for some miles, we alight to make the ascent to the crater on foot. Then appears another swarm of beggars to assist you up the steep mountain and through the rugged sweep of loose masses of pumice-stone. They evidently want to render some assistance, so I finally arrange with one of them to pull me up with a rope. Another comes along and pushes at my back, while others want to get a chair, etc., all for pay, of course; but I conclude that one is enough. He finally balks, and says, in broken English, "I no horse." He banters me to hire the others to help. I leave him, and tell him that I have no need of him. Finally he goes on, and after numerous halts for a new bargain, etc., we get half the way up. The others drop off, and I am not annoyed any more.

As we reach the top of Vesuvius we see the sulphur all around us and smell the hellish compounds, which are almost unendurable. The fire and smoke and terrible rumbling sounds, as if an outbreak or eruption were about to take place, come from a hillock in the shape of a cone, one hundred feet high, forming the center of the crater, and which is surrounded by a circular ditch about two hundred feet deep and five hundred feet wide, whose inner wall is, I should think, a mile in circumference, which bounds the outer area of the crater. The sulphur coating the cone, from which the smoke and fire are emitted, is of a brilliant and beautiful color. The molten lava lies seething at the bottom of the cone, and as the terrible sounds belch forth, it would seem the wisest part of valor to hurry away, if ever we would see our friends in Columbus again; but the guides inform us that there is "no danger." A copper coin is put into a stream of melted lava, and we bring away with us a piece of it with the imprint. The view below us is superb. The beautiful bay, as it gracefully curves around toward Naples, the distant villas on the mountain-sides, the islands of Capri and Ischia, the far-stretching sea, the city itself, with its half million population, its beautiful suburbs covered with vineyards, and Pompeii and Herculaneum beneath us, well repay us for all our trouble in ascending the mountain on this terribly hot day; nevertheless, we get a refreshing, cooling breeze from the sea. We descend, plunging our feet and legs knee-deep into the *debris* at every step, like walking in cinders. When we get back to where our horses are stationed and pay our guide, he beseeches us in pitiful tones for more, although we had paid him well; and so he continues to follow us with others until, in order to get rid of them, we put our horses to full speed and escape.

In regard to the annoyances which are sometimes encountered in Italian travel, the experience of a Boston clergyman, whom we met at breakfast in Rome, may furnish our readers a vivid example. He was traveling by rail to Naples, having with him Cook's tickets, which entitled him to a seat in a second-class car. He was the only foreigner in the compartment, the companions around him being exceedingly rough and drunken Italians, so that he really feared robbery and assassination. At the first station he alighted and took a seat in a first-class carriage or car, intending, when the conductor came round, to pay the difference between the charges of the first and second class vehicles, the charge for the former being about a third higher than for the latter. When his ticket was called for, however, he was roughly compelled to pay full fare and give up his Cook's excursion tickets, covering the expenses of his route through Europe and his journey home, and then locked into the compartment. Failing to make any one understand a single word he uttered, he feared that he should lose his tickets, not even knowing the name of the station where the guard left him. On his arrival at Naples, through the assistance of the American Consul, and after great difficulty, he at length succeeded in recovering his tickets. His experience also with the guides in ascending Vesuvius was frightful. They succeeded in fleecing him out of twenty-five dollars, because he neglected to make his contract with them in advance, and every man who could get an opportunity to assist him in any way compelled him to pay. He seemed to be glad that he had escaped with his life. It is not safe to undertake such a trip alone, and it is necessary always to make every contract in advance and to shake off every attempt to render you assistance except from your own proper guide, no matter from whom else it may be.

An Italian railroad is slow enough in comparison with the roads in America and Great Britain. They do not average more than twelve or fifteen miles an hour, and stop a long time at every station. It is amusing to see a number of officials inspect the carriages before starting and lock the doors, and then, if any one is missing, wait any length of time for him. Before starting they ring a little bell, then examine the coaches to see if all are aboard. Then the guard cries out "Go on!" and finally some one on the engine blows a tin horn, very like the dinner-horn used by our farmers, and in a few minutes off we go.

We had an intelligent guide who took us over Pompeii. It was built, according to history, about six hundred years before Christ. At the time of its destruction it was occupied by the Romans, and on the twenty-fourth day of August, A. D. 79, was swallowed up, as well as Herculaneum, by an eruption of Vesuvius. The terrible visitation lasted three days. Here Pliny the Elder lost his life, and his nephew, Pliny the Younger, gives a graphic account of the total catastrophe of the city's overthrow. Our guide informed us that a population of nearly half a million had formerly resided here; but he is evidently wrong, if we may judge from the size of the city remaining, as well as from the idea generally received that it was a place of but third-rate importance. The people were mostly at the theater, probably witnessing some grand gladiatorial show, when the storm of destruction fell upon them; and from the small number of skeletons excavated, it is supposed that most of the inhabitants made their escape. It is not many years since this wondrous city was to any great extent uncovered, with its regular streets, its buildings, public and private, its frescoed walls, its beautiful statuary and its numerous theaters and places of amusement, showing the devotion of its inhabitants to business, art and pleasure. The prevailing architecture was Greek. The private houses had only two floors, and were built nearly upon the same model, while the rooms were small and covered with profuse decoration. The streets are narrow, laid with flat paving-stones, and ruts worn in them by the chariot wheels, drawn by slaves, are plainly to be seen, as well as the worn stones put down at the crossings for pedestrians. The shops and houses were adorned with mosaics and with pictures. We walked through the streets until we were tired, looking at these quaint remains, indicative of their ancient habits and customs. Now we read the inscriptions upon the walls and over the doors of their residences, nearly two thousand years buried in the earth. Sad is the story that many of them reveal, showing that prostitution was undoubtedly barefaced and respectable in this luxurious and brilliant city, for signs by pictures and terribly vulgar devices over many a door on the main streets invited the inhabitants to enter these dens of infamy. Everything around us is curious, wonderful and ancient, and it may readily be seen that art held a high place among these people—pagans of the ancient world.

Sunday, in Naples, in our hotel, situated close by the bay, with a fine old castle standing out in the water, making a lovely scene, was a period of rest which we were glad to enjoy, having just accomplished the hardest week's work of any since we left home; for it strains one's mind and nerves to behold so great a variety of scenes which awaken wonder and admiration. We are glad to turn our faces homeward. Our journey now is northward through Florence, Venice, Germany, Holland, etc., with the hope of being home early in

September, or earlier if we can secure passage, which it is almost impossible to do except one engages return tickets, as we did, on the steamer by which we came over.

XVI.

FLORENCE, THE CITY OF PALACES.... THE DUOMO AND CAMPANILE.... ART COLLECTIONS AT THE UFFIZI PALACE ..THE STUDIO OF POWERS .. "THE BRIDE OF THE SEA".... A GONDOLA TRIP THROUGH VENICE ... PALACE OF THE DOGES, SAN MARCO AND CLOCK TOWER. ... PIAZZA OF ST. MARK ... EVENING RECREATIONS.

Venice, Italy.

FROM Naples to Venice our road lay through the fig, almond and olive orchards and lovely vineyards, with vines gracefully festooned from tree to tree, showing the principal articles cultivated in Italy. At this time of year the ground looks parched and arid, and without tarrying long at any place we are glad to get farther north and stop at Florence, the "fairest city in the world."

Florence, the old Tuscan capital, stands in the valley of the Arno, a river whose glories have been celebrated in many a poet's song, and whose scenes have been reproduced by many an artist's pencil. At this late season, the close of the summer months, it is a muddy, sluggish stream, about the size of our own Scioto. Crossing it are six bridges, and on the streets bordering its banks are located many of the best hotels and residences, and when shown to our rooms it was announced to us that we had a look-out upon the Arno. Florence is a city of churches, palaces, studios, etc., and to examine all the beautiful works of art would make necessary a lengthened stay. The Duomo, or Cathedral, is the first object of interest that the traveler generally seeks. One is disappointed on first entering the edifice, for it is dark and gloomy as we come in from the exceedingly bright sunshine without; but we soon get accustomed to the scene, and enjoy the soft and tender beauty of the light streaming through the windows. The dome is said to be the widest in the world. When Michael Angelo was engaged upon the plan of St. Peter's and was told that he had now an opportunity of surpassing the dome of Florence, he replied: "I will make her sister dome larger, yes.—but not more beautiful."

After seeing St. Peter's one is not in a condition at once to look with much interest upon other cathedrals, since he has already seen the greatest and noblest in the world. The exterior of the Florentine Duomo is composed of marbles of many colors, giving the building a rich and brilliant appearance under the midday sun. The bell-towers of Italy often stand by themselves apart from the churches, as does the famous campanile of this cathedral. The great artist Giotto, the "Shepherd-Boy of Fiesole," was the architect, and it seems almost perfect, with its variegated marbles rising to the height of two hundred and ninety-three feet. Ruskin says: "This is the model and mirror of perfect architecture"; and Longfellow, in his description of it, says:

> "In the old Tuscan town stands Giotto's tower,
> The lily of Florence, blossoming in stone,—
> A vision, a delight, and a desire,—
> The builder's perfect and centennial flower."

We must not leave Florence without visiting the "Galleria degli Uffizi," and see especially the fine groups of statuary having a world-wide celebrity.

We had so often seen copies of the Venus di Medici, and heard it referred to as the most beautiful embodiment of female loveliness in the world, that it was a delight to examine and re-examine so masterly a rendering in marble of all that is pure and lovely in woman,—quite in contrast to the "Venus of the Capitol" in Rome, which has a robust and sensual appearance. This *chef-d'œuvre* of art was brought from Tivoli, near Rome, to Florence, in 1680, and although much marred and broken, still retains its pre-eminence in the realm of art. The Apollino, the Wrestlers, the Grinder, the Dancing Faun, are all, I believe, productions of ancient art, and are wonderfully life-like. Here are sculptures and paintings by the foremost artists of all time—Raphael, Titian, Michael Angelo, Leonardo da Vinci and others; but I do not pretend to an artistic training sufficient to pronounce upon their merits. We visited the studio of Powers, who, it will be remembered, was for some time a resident of Ohio (Cincinnati), and who for many years resided here in Florence, where he gained a reputation as the greatest of modern sculptors. His wife still maintains the studio, where she lives, just outside the city gates. During our call there, his oldest son, a native of Cincinnati, kindly showed us the sculptures of his father,—the "Greek Slave," etc. Mr. Powers left three sons and three daughters, who are still living in Florence. The sons, I believe, have all somewhat of their father's genius, and models were shown us, now in process of development, as well as works of merit already completed by them. One of the daughters, also, is an artist. One of the sons has a photographic establishment near by, in which he makes a specialty of photographing his father's works. He also produces photographic views about Florence, and few cities in the world have so picturesque and grand a location, spreading out as it does through its environs upon surrounding hills, where are seen beautiful villas on the ways leading toward Vallombrosa and in other directions. We obtained a splendid evening view of the city from the Tower of Galileo, where we see the villa in which he spent the closing years of his life, and where he was visited by Milton. Americans, it is said, are fast taking possession of Florence, and they claim that they can live much more cheaply here than in the United States; but how any one, without some other reason than this, can expatriate himself from his country and friends, I cannot understand.

We know that we are approaching Venice, the "Bride of the Sea," as we come in sight of and cross the lagoons, the most famous in Europe. Venice is a city of islands. Of these there are no less than one hundred and seventeen, united by nearly four hundred bridges. As we arrive at the depot we are met by the gondoliers of the different hotels, and at once get seated in one of their black, graceful conveyances, where new scenes and sights meet us on every hand. Every few moments we think we are going to be run into by gondolas coming from every direction, often with only one oarsman with his one solitary oar, which he plies upon one side only of his boat; but we soon gain confidence, as our gondolier turns the sharp corners, just missing the wall or the prow of some on-coming neighbor, and, as he plies his one loose oar with wonderful dexterity, calling out in his musical Italian, "*Già è—già è!*" (Boat ahead—boat ahead!) Canals take the place of streets, and the gondola is the only vehicle that runs upon these watery avenues. Neither horse nor carriage of any kind is in Venice, which now contains one hundred and thirty thousand inhabitants, although in the fifteenth century, when it was the focus of the entire commerce of Europe, its population numbered two hundred thousand. The palaces and business houses front on the canals, and run back to a little narrow foot-walk, from five to six feet wide, and all the carrying business is done in gondolas; indeed, it is almost impossible to get about the city in any other way. We meet the business man reading his paper, the market-man with his load of fish and vegetables, and the various bustle and stir of the city, and finally alight at our hotel. We find its marble steps partly covered with water, and our rooms overlooking the Grand Canal, which is the main artery of the city and nearly two miles long. There are one hundred and forty-seven canals (or streets) in all. The Adriatic Sea gleams in the distance; and, nearer at hand, the Lido and other islands, whence come the fresh vegetables for the market, for there are no gardens or green shrubs in Venice. The houses are all built by driving down substantial piles under the entire building, and in time the foundations become petrified and as solid as stone.

ST. MARK'S PLACE, VENICE.

We undertake a voyage through Venice. As it is impossible to walk to the bank to get our letters, we find it necessary to hire for the day a gondolier, for whose services we pay one dollar and thirty cents. We land at the steps of the bank, and float all day from place to place in these luxurious boats, restful and easy, and, refreshed by a delightful sea-breeze, quite in contrast with the hot, dry air of southern Italy, we enjoy it with a zeal unequaled since we left home. We meet in the afternoon and evening the private gondolas, handsomely fitted up, filled with families taking their daily airing, or the lady alone making her calls and arranging her toilet at her mirror before alighting at her neighbor's door; and at moonlight the lovers, blissful and alone, enjoying the cool breeze away from the eyes of the jealous ones—conducive, I should think, to quick engagements. We visit at evening one of the islands, and return by the long range of hotels and palaces fronting the sea, affording one of the most splendid views in the world. Queen Marguerite had just alighted at the king's palace, and the handsome gondoliers were happy in being, as they thought, so highly honored as to be employed by the royal family. The new king, Humbert, and his handsome queen seem to be adored by the people. He has a sober, solemn face, without marked features. We visited the wonderful Palace of the Doges, founded in the year 800, and then the historic halls—that of the Grand Council, the Hall of Elections, the Hall of the Senate, etc., etc., adorned with the choicest paintings, and cross the "Bridge of Sighs," to which so much interest is attached through the exquisite lines of Byron:

> "I stood in Venice, on the Bridge of Sighs,—
> A palace and a prison on each hand."

We see in the Sala delle Scudo, or "Hall of the Shield," a "map of the world by Fra Mauro," made in 1457 (with the American Continent left out)—the greatest curiosity of its kind in the world. Also we see Titian's famous picture, "The Assumption," and so many old monuments, sculptures, paintings, etc., etc., that one wearies at the very thought of remembering a one-thousandth part of them.

The old Church of San Marco, with its five domes, is wonderful, the interior looking as if it were a "vast cave hewn out into the form of a cross, and divided into shadowy aisles by many pillars." The floors are of marble, and are so worn and uneven as to be difficult to walk over. They claim that the body of St. Mark the Evangelist rests here, brought from Alexandria. Whether true or not, he is the patron saint of Venice, and the present magnificent edifice owes its origin to the advent of the sacred relics. We ascended the Campanile, three hundred and four feet in height, by means of a winding inclined plane, and from the summit enjoyed a commanding view of the city, the sea and the Italian Alps. At two o'clock we visited the Clock Tower in the piazza of St. Mark, to witness the feeding of the pigeons. On the platform in front stand two Vulcans in bronze, who strike the hours on bells, when immediately a large flock of pigeons fly down, daily at this hour, to be fed at the expense of the city. According to tradition, Admiral Enrico Dandolo, while besieging Candia, at the beginning of the thirteenth century, received intelligence from the island, by means of carrier-pigeons, which greatly facilitated its conquest. He then dispatched the birds to Venice with the news of his success, and since that period they have been carefully tended and highly revered by the citizens. No one injures or frightens them, and they are tame and happy about this busy square when being fed.

In the evening we groped our way from the rear of our hotel through the narrow walks to the piazza of St. Mark, the central place of attraction when the military bands play. We found thousands of the Venetians of all classes, from the prince to the beggar, enjoying the fresh air and sauntering up and down, while some were indulging in refreshments in front of the *cafés*. Many of the ladies were beautifully dressed, and were both graceful and handsome. It was an animated scene—the Procuratie, St. Mark's, the Palace of the Doges, the Piazzetta, and the lagoons by moonlight, together with the crowds of people, the brilliant lights, and over all the splendid Italian sky. The piazza is rectangular, ninety yards in breadth by one hundred and ninety-two in length, and paved with blocks of trachyte and marble, and on three sides inclosed by splendid marble palaces, blackened through age and long exposure to the weather. The stores and shop-windows are full of diamonds, rich jewelry and pictures, and we obtain a realizing sense of the dazzling gayety of Venetian life. The people of Naples, Rome and Venice, and, indeed, all over the Continent, seem to be bent on enjoying themselves, and are ever out of doors in the cool of the evening, in great crowds, around the *cafés*, parks and places of amusement. In Naples, on Sunday evenings, the streets and public squares are brilliantly lighted, giving the city the appearance of some grand illumination.

XVII.

THE OLD AMPHITHEATER AT VERONA....DEPARTURE FROM ITALY....TRENT....GERMAN HOMELIKENESS....MUNICH ....THE PINAKOTHEK....FAMOUS AMERICANS IN BRONZE ....THE GREAT BREWERIES....USE OF STIMULANTS.... A NOVEL SPECIES OF MORGUE....FAMOUS CEMETERIES OF EUROPE....HEIDELBERG AND ITS STUDENTS.

Heidelberg, Germany.

WE have now been about eight hundred miles through Italy, down by the eastern and returning by the middle-western side, *via* Verona, to Germany, and everywhere have been greatly interested. Italy is overflowing with objects of interest, historical and artistic, and if with "united Italy" comes, as there should, a stable government, with its consequent prosperity, this historic peninsula must again become a power in the world. We have found throughout splendid hotels, with reasonable charges. They have invariably marble floors and stairs—no carpets—and the rooms are often elegantly furnished. Here we found, for the first time in Europe, plenty of fruit—grapes, figs, peaches, plums and apples—cheaper than in Ohio. The fall and spring would be much more delightful seasons to visit Italy than July, August or September; but we have enjoyed the sights and scenes, so new to us, exceedingly, and take our leave of them after a visit to Verona, the second of the quadrilateral cities, heavily fortified and near the Austrian frontier. The great curiosity in this place is the Roman Amphitheater, in so much better preservation than the Coliseum at Rome. It was probably built under Diocletian, about A. D. 284, and it is said to have seated over twenty thousand spectators and to have been capable of holding seventy thousand. Every row of seats is still unbroken, although the building was erected in the third century. Nowadays in its corridors various trades are being carried on, such as blacksmithing, wagon-making, etc., a pleasing contrast, in peaceful industry, to the wild and turbulent scenes once witnessed in these ancient passages; whilst above and below ground are winding ways, bringing vividly to mind the thousands hurrying in and out, intent upon the bloody spectacles of the arena. During our visit there, a theatrical troupe was performing (perhaps "Romeo and Juliet") in a frame theater built within the walls, from the tops of which we could see the actors, but could not hear the play. The prima donna, as advertised on the bills, was Catharina Howard (we wondered if Italian theatrical stars in Italy assume English names, as ours so often assume Italian ones in America). In Verona, it will be remembered, are laid most of the scenes of Shakespeare's "Romeo and Juliet" (the chief incidents of which were of actual occurrence), as well as the scenes of the "Two Gentlemen of Verona," and various other plays and romances by other authors. Juliet's tomb is pointed out in the Garden of the Orfanotrofio, "notable as being the lady so immortalized first by Da Porto in the novel, and afterward and so unapproachably by Shakespeare." We notice a great many soldiers around the city and public squares, and learn that there is a garrison of six thousand men at the base of the Alps. The city contains a population of sixty thousand, but looks poverty-stricken and dilapidated, though heavily fortified, while large forts are to be seen all around on the neighboring hills.

We now leave Italy and enter Austria at Ala, where all are marched out of the cars to have their baggage examined. We pass the city of Trent, specially celebrated as the scene of the sessions of the "Great Council of Trent" in 1545-63, and continue our journey through the wild valley of the Eisack, with noble fortifications and ancient castles on every hand. We ascend the Alps through the Brenner Pass. The tunnels are very numerous, and the curves and precipices so bold and fearful as almost to make one shudder. At Innspruck the scenery of the valley becomes very grand. Our baggage is again examined at Sterzing, where we cross over the frontier into Germany, and it seems as if we were again in "God's country," among our friends, as we see the strong, broad, German faces, and hear the German language everywhere spoken. We have so many Germans in Columbus among our best citizens that we are greatly interested in their native country, and with the sprinkling of

German words at our command can manage to talk enough to be understood. Coming from the heated air and dry and parched plains and uplands of Italy to the green fields and salubrious climate of Germany is exhilarating in the extreme, and we enjoy the wide meadows, splendid farm-houses and substantial appearance of everything. Wherever the railroad crosses a turnpike, a beam (painted blue and white like a barber's pole) is stretched across the highway and carefully closed whenever a train approaches.

Munich challenges all the other capitals of Europe for beauty, and rivals Paris or Rome as a repository of art. We ride and walk about the splendid old city of over two hundred thousand inhabitants, with its beautiful public and private buildings, numerous parks and clean streets, which Maximilian I., Louis I. and Louis II. did so much to build up and foster, and furnish with the finest productions of art and science. The celebrated Munich bronze foundry and stained-glass manufactory are located here, and our intelligent old guide, proud of his native city, showed us the picture-galleries of the royal palaces, old and new (the royal palaces in Bavaria are called residences), and the old and new Pinakothek (gallery of pictures). The latter was specially interesting, as the paintings were all productions of modern artists, and I was anxious to see something besides the works of the old masters, of which we have seen so much in Rome, Florence and Venice. In one of the rooms the guide took great interest in showing us the likenesses of King Louis, his wife and ten children. This king seems to be exceedingly popular with the Bavarians, while they chafe under the present rule and look forward for a day of deliverance. Now they have to help support the German government, and pay also a large amount to keep up the royal household of Louis.

At the bronze foundry are the original models for the statues of many distinguished Americans. The guide pointed out to me a model, saying, with emphasis, "This is General Washington; next that is —what you call him?—oh, President Lincoln, the *black man.*" There were also models of Webster, Marshall, Clay, Benton, Grant, Peabody and many other of our great men, and one feels proud of the appearance of American statesmen, etc., at the side of those of other nations. The proprietor of the foundry informed me that they had more orders for the statue of Lincoln than for any other. Statues of Humboldt and Shakespeare were being molded while we were there — an order from St. Louis. Americans are the best patrons. They speak proudly of the Tyler Davidson fountain, cast here, as being one of the finest in the world. This fountain is a gift from Mr. Henry Probasco, a citizen of Cincinnati, to the people of that place. The cost amounted to one hundred and seventy-five thousand dollars, and the bronze work weighs twenty-four tons. Forty-five tons of porphyry rest solidly on the bottom of the basin, and its rim contains forty tons of the same beautiful material. All this was quarried and dressed in the Kingdom of Saxony, and shipped to this country unmarred by break or scratch. This fountain constitutes the art feature of Cincinnati, perhaps even of the western world, and will well repay, to art lovers desirous of seeing it, the trouble even of a long and tedious journey. When it was first put up on the grounds of the foundry, over four thousand inhabitants of Munich were present to see it play.

But we must not leave Munich without seeing

the great breweries, beer-houses and beer-gardens. Of the former there are fifteen or twenty large ones and about the same number of smaller ones. Some of them cover five or six acres, and the great beer-cellars underground, hewn out in some rocky eminence, with their one hundred thousand barrels of beer, give one an idea of its daily consumption in this city. We pass the "Bavaria Keller," one of the most frequented, on an eminence overlooking the large race-course and park, and a splendid panorama of the mountains and surrounding country, where thousands assemble on pleasant evenings— all classes, men, women and children, bringing their cheese, ham, sausages and bread with them, and enjoying the refreshing draught of lager, with a band of music playing. We went into the Hofbrauhaus (King's Brewery), crowded with men and women, drinking and chatting and making a bedlam equal to the Bourse in Paris or the Gold Room in New York. Women and girls were coming and going, crowding their way along among the men with their mugs and their wire casters, holding from three to six glasses of the foaming beverage. The guide asked me to take a glass of beer. I declined.

He continued: "I don't want any now; I always prepare myself by eating something before drinking." He says that everybody in Germany, men, women and children, drink beer and wine, and that sometimes one establishment has the run of custom, and then, if they do not keep up to the standard of good beer, and somebody else makes better, all rush off to their new favorite. Everywhere in Europe the exception is not to drink at table, and waiters would hand us the wine list and ask us, "What will you have?" "Nothing." Then they would say: "No beer, no wine?" In Great Britain people drink brown stout and ale; in France, wine and absinthe; in Switzerland and Italy, wine; in Germany, beer and wine. An American gentleman was invited to dine with a distinguished professor of Trinity College, Cambridge, England, and he asked the professor, "Don't you have water on your table?" "Why, no; I never drank water in my life."

At the beautiful cemetery (Gottesacker) a novel sight was presented. Inside the grounds stood a large building, with marble floors, and arches supported by columns, divided into three spacious rooms, fronted with large panes of glass, all of them facing the inside of a quadrangle. In front of these windows, and in full view of the visitors, lay the dead, covered with flowers. The rooms are divided into first, second, and third class departments (the former being a large one), according to the standing and wealth of the deceased. When any one dies in Munich they are taken at once in a carriage to one of these rooms, without being accompanied by their friends, who afterward follow and decorate the body with flowers. In some of the rooms, candles were burning by the dead. In one room alone were children of all ages. Their faces looked like marble in their beautiful repose, decked as they were with lovely flowers. In the third-class room there were bodies without any floral decoration. No doubt their families were too poor to bear the expense. The bodies must remain in these rooms for the space of forty-eight hours. A fine wire is attached to the forefinger of each body, and goes to a room near by, where bells, which are numbered, are attached to the separate wires, while watchers are continually present. The slightest motion from any body exposed, so delicate are these wires, would instantly ring a bell, so that if a bell strikes the watchers know that there has been a movement in some body in the adjoining room, and they run at once to see if any person lying there is still alive, and to apply the proper remedies for their resuscitation. After the forty-eight hours have expired, notice is given in the public papers, and friends come and place the body in a tomb or in the ground; but to have a dear friend's body thus exposed to the common gaze appears to me extremely repulsive. It reminds one too much of the morgue in Paris, where the suicides are exposed to view, with all their clothes and a description of the body hung up at the window, that friends may come and claim them.

Perhaps one of the most lovely tributes which we pay to departed friends is the decoration of our cemeteries. Throughout our land they blossom and bloom,—fields of consolation, God's acres, indeed; but in Europe they are often of a different description—gorgeous and magnificent, perhaps, in sepulchral decoration, but lacking that tender solicitude and care, that sweet home feeling embracing the very dead, which are characteristic of our lovely cemeteries at home. Near the barriers of Paris lies one, crowded and gloomy, but with a world-wide fame — Père la Chaise. It is situated on the highest point within the city limits, completely covered with dark, dismal tombs, with narrow walks winding around them, reminding one of the Catacombs. Hung upon the tombs are wreaths of immortelles or of bead-work, and, allowed to remain until blackened and decayed, they present a sad and forbidding sight. The Campo Santo in Genoa, on the contrary, is one of the most beautiful cemeteries of its peculiar style I ever saw. Its whole arrangement is unique and interesting. It contains some ten acres of ground, surrounded by a rotunda, with marble floor and columns over the vaults. In the rear of this rotunda are niches for marble statuary, and when any person has died who is to be here interred, beautiful marble sculpture, either in the bust or the full form, is placed in these niches — sometimes erect and sometimes in a reclining position, as when laid in the tomb. There is also an internal gallery, and the whole building in the upper tier is supported by monolithic columns of black marble, and no expense seems to have been spared in making this cemetery the most costly of any in the world, and, as we have above said, entirely unique. Pisa also contains a famous Campo Santo. It was founded in 1188, and has three chapels attached to it. The walls are covered with frescoes by artists of the fourteenth and fifteenth centuries, and it is wonderful for the age in which it was built. In Pompeii the old burial-place is still to be seen, and, singularly enough, it contains tombstones much like those in our own beautiful Green Lawn. In Rome, besides the catacombs and tombs everywhere encountered among the ruins, are also large tombs or excavations in the ground, over which stand stone buildings, with vases placed in niches in the wall (around a stone rotunda), with the Roman name upon the vases, which contain the ashes of the dead, showing that cremation is no new thing. The English Cemetery in Rome is beautifully laid out, according to modern style. Here lie the mortal remains of Keats and Shelley:

> "And gray walls moulder round, on which dull Time
> Feeds, like slow fire upon a hoary brand."

Heidelberg, where we now are, is a splendid city, with its very old university, its far older castle, and its most picturesque surroundings. We see the German students here, with their robust forms and intellectual faces, and it is noticeable that so many of them, old and young, wear glasses, that we came to the conclusion that it must be a popular custom, as indicating the student and scholar. An English student whom I met here said to me, "Do you notice the cuts on the faces of the young men? Every little while, to settle some difficulty, they go out with their friends and take it out with short swords." He said, moreover, that they were inveterate beer-drinkers, and would take from ten to twenty glasses in an evening, and that he could not bear to have them come to his room, they were so personally offensive through the combined odors of beer and tobacco-smoke.

XVIII.

Degradation of the Female Peasantry on the Continent.... A Sunday in Heidelberg... The Old Castle and the University.... A Land of Plenty ...Frankfort-on-the-Main.... The Judengasse.... Antiquities of the City....Down the Rhine.... Cologne and its Cathedral....Thoughts upon Art.

Paris, France.

THE women on the Continent seem to have a hard time — I mean the lower class. In Switzerland we saw them drawing heavy loads and carrying on their backs, up the mountain-steeps, deep, burdensome baskets, and even harnessed with a cow to a cart. In one instance a cow and a man on the one side, and a woman on the other, were drawing a load. The cow having become frightened at the railroad train, they were in danger of being run away with, and were holding on to her horns.

In Munich, women were the hod-carriers, bearing great loads of mortar and brick wherever building was going on, and in Heidelberg they were carrying long, heavy bars of iron on their shoulders. With us the iron would have been carried on drays. All women and children appear to drink wine and beer as freely as the men, and have their glasses of wine at the hotels; but nowhere on the Continent do we remember to have seen a person drunk or quarrelsome.

At Heidelberg we attended worship at the old Church of the Holy Ghost, whither we were directed to go, under the information that we should there find service conducted by the Presbyterian Church of Scotland; but unexpectedly found ourselves in a Roman Catholic church. We thought that we had not been understood in our inquiry, and were next pointed in another direction, where Church of England service was held. On our way we met a good old Scotch Presbyterian family from our hotel, and thinking that they were going to church, followed them, and, to our surprise, they entered the same church we had previously found occupied by the Roman Catholics, and here we discovered the Scotch minister, perched up in a little pulpit far away from his audience, which consisted of about twenty worshipers. I found this old church had the odd peculiarity of being partitioned through the center, so that the Romanists held service at one end, and at the same time the Protestants at the other. I had at first entered the wrong division. Heidelberg is a Protestant city, and the Lutherans here have splendid, capacious churches, and large audiences on Sabbath mornings; although, as I walked the main street, I noticed that stores and banks were open, and the general appearance was rather like some holiday, as the people were loitering about and well-dressed. The old Church of St. Peter, where Jerome of Prague, the reformer, hurled his defiance to the Papacy, is still standing.

The grand old castle of Heidelberg, fulfilling my preconceived ideas of a castle, is situated "high on the forehead of Jettenbühl," with mountains behind and in front. From the broad terrace of masonry you can almost throw a stone upon the roofs of the town, so closely do they lie below this massive, half-ruined structure, with its octagon and its round and square towers, battered and shattered by the mace

HEIDELBERG CASTLE.

of war. It is said to be the most magnificent ruin of the Middle Ages. The University, with its celebrated schools of law and medicine, whose professional chairs have been adorned by many noted scholars, and where some of our own young Americans have studied, is a building plain and unpretentious. The students are divided into five different corps, distinguished by the color of their caps— Prussian, white; Rhinelander, blue; etc.

All the way from Heidelberg to Frankfort (indeed, wherever we have been in Germany), like the land of Canaan, the country seems to flow with milk and honey—a land of corn and wine, of beautiful fields and steep slopes, terraced and green with vineyards. So precipitous and rugged are the hill-sides that oftentimes it seems almost impossible to ascend them. The country does not produce the olive, but large quantities of oil are procured from the walnut, the poppy, and from rape-seed. There are no fences or hedges to their fields. The ox and the heifer are yoked together, and whole families, without regard to sex, are seen busy gathering the wheat and barley and cultivating the vineyards.

Frankfort-on-the-Main is a great commercial city,

and looks, as you approach it, like a splendid capital; and as one rides through the beautiful streets, it is noticeable that all the houses are of a neutral tint. We asked Captain Lee, our efficient, gentlemanly American Consul (once of the Ohio *State Journal*), to whom we are indebted for valuable attentions, what was the meaning of it. He replied: "It is a part of the municipal law of the city that all houses must have only the neutral colors." The different colors were like the stone of Chittenden's block (corner of High and Spring streets, Columbus), and gave the thoroughfares of the city a neat and unusual appearance, reminding us, also, of the cream-colored stone fronts of Paris. Before the Exposition, Paris passed a law requiring all house-owners to clean off the fronts of their houses, which well accounts for the fresh, tidy look of all the streets; and there is a municipal law requiring this to be done throughout the city every seven years. Frankfort is one of the great money centers of the world, and was the first foreign city to take our Government bonds, of which it now holds one hundred millions. After the passage of the Silver Bill, many of the smaller bond-holders here returned them to the United

States, and now are chagrined and astonished that they were taken up so readily by our own people. All the banks, including that of the Rothschilds, are plain-looking buildings with iron gratings at the windows, giving them the appearance of jails.

In the Judengasse, or Jews' Alley, Rothschild's first banking-room was shown us. It is about eight feet by ten, without a window — only a door; and over this entrance now were a few old boots hung up for sale. From 1460 until within a few years, all the Jews were compelled to reside here, and the thoroughfare was closed by gates at each end all night and on Sundays and holidays. These old, dingy, antiquated houses have beheld many a dark scene of Jewish persecution and suffering. Now, many of this once oppressed and downtrodden people live in the most splendid palaces and mansions in the city, and we hope that the days of Jewish persecution throughout the world are over.

We stop to look at the old, slate-covered house called "Lutherhaus," where Luther preached from the balcony when on his way to Worms. It bears his portrait and the inscription, "*In silentio et spe erit fortitudo vestra.*" The Römer, or Town Hall, is an antiquated-looking building with three gables. In the hall of this building are the frescoed portraits of the emperors of Germany, and within the edifice twenty-four emperors, counting from the first, have been crowned. Goethe seems to be the god which the Frankforters worship, and the house where he was born, in 1749, has this inscription: "In Diesem Hause wurde Johann Wolfgang Goethe, am 28 August, 1749, Geboren." For two miles we rode through and around beautiful parks in the center of the city. Captain Lee lives on one of the best streets, in the vicinity of other consuls, but in plain, republican simplicity, quite in contrast with their splendid residences. His family speak German fluently, and we hope he will not turn "Dutchman," but re-turn to the Ohio *State Journal* again. Ever since we have crossed the Alps, and also on the Alps at Innspruck, we have met rain. We have had occasional showers almost every day, though we had not seen rain in Italy for a month, and Captain Lee informed us that it rains almost daily here, more or less, throughout the season.

We have promise of a beautiful day at Mayence for our trip down the Rhine, and with great anticipations we take the steamer for Cologne and proceed on our way, with the bridge of boats connecting Mayence and Cassel in full view above us. Gliding between the islands and passing many towns and villas, we soon come to the hill-sides, terraced with green vineyards, where, perched on the top of some rock or steep hill, are seen the old castles, some in ruins and others restored and inhabited. To each one appertains some interesting legend, which is entertaining to read as we sweep along so coolly and delightfully, after our diversified and somewhat toilsome trip through Italy. On a rocky island in the midst of the river stands the Mäusethurm, or Mouse Tower. A strange legend, which has been versified by Southey, connects the tower with a certain Bishop Hatto, who, for hoarding corn which the starving people needed, and burning in a barn a number of them who complained, was devoured in this tower, whither he had taken refuge, by an army of mice. Every little while, in a turn of the river, some grand old castle meets our view, and all day long we are kept on the lookout for new scenes and the fresh interest excited by the legends connected with them.

I was disappointed in the Rhine scenery, and, were

it not for the unusual sight of so many old castles (I think I counted some twenty-five in number) and the legends with which this stream is thronged, it would be found less interesting than the Hudson, which far surpasses it in picturesque beauty. It possesses nothing to compare with the scenery at West Point and many other places on our American river, —not even in the far-famed rocks of the Lurlei. The towns and villas are not so beautiful, and were it not for the vineyards on the hill-sides, terraced and green, the river banks would present but a barren appearance. It is said that in some places the soil is deposited on these precipitous hill-sides by manual labor, and ranged in terraces built on the face of the rock, and which are so difficult of access that to reach them much risk is incurred by the laborers of both sexes. It pays well, however, to cultivate the grape here, on account of the fame of the Rhenish wines all over the world.

The Cathedral at Cologne is one of the most famous in the world, and by walking around its exterior and viewing it from different standpoints one gets an idea of the magnificence of the whole and the exquisite beauty of some of the details. The interior, with its grand forest of columns, as you gaze down the aisle with its massive pillars for four hundred feet, is wonderfully grand. The two towers are not yet finished; the work is still in progress, and, when completed, this cathedral will be among the highest and most perfect in proportions and beauty of any in existence. Though, to my mind, St. Peter's, at Rome, seems as perfect in its architectural proportions as any monument of art can be. As you stand at the foot of Mont Blanc, in Switzerland, or on Inspiration Point, in California, commanding a view of the Yosemite, you realize something of God's majesty and power; so, as you walk through St. Peter's, in Rome, you feel that this is the grandest work of art that man has ever produced, and that Michael Angelo, the builder of its dome, was a wonder of God's power, as developed in his great versatility and astonishing genius.

We saw in Venice the first painting of Titian, when at the age of twelve, and his last, in his one hundredth year. The latter was not finished at his death. The Milan Cathedral is the most beautiful and elaborate of all we have seen, with its forest of turrets and thousands of statues in the niches and on pedestals, decorating its whole exterior. When the two towers of the Cologne Cathedral are finished, it will take its rank as third in reputation in the world. We have seen the most famous paintings in Europe. The best known of all is the "Cenacolo," or "Last Supper," by Leonardo da Vinci, the painter, sculptor, musician, mathematician and man of science, in the Convent of Santa Maria delle Grazie, in Milan. The picture is twenty-eight feet in length, and no other work is so often praised and so often copied. This greatest of all paintings is on the damp wall of the old refectory, and is now almost obliterated. The artist was many years painting it. I never thought that the expression given to Our Saviour by most of the great painters could be anything like the original, according to my conception of his character. Most of them have given him a sad and feminine look, with regularly formed and small features, instead of making his countenance the index of the strong character appropriate to the greatest and godliest of men; and from what we learn of the private characteristics of some of these painters of Christ, the Madonnas, the Assumption, Crucifixion, Immaculate Conception, etc., we should judge that they could not have been greatly capable of conceiving his true character, or of an inspiration to do justice to the delineation of Him who was the greatest among ten thousand and altogether lovely.

Cologne is a large city, of one hundred and fifty thousand inhabitants,—the largest in the Rhenish province of Prussia. The expulsion of the Jews and other events in the fifteenth century, when it was almost unexampled in prosperity, caused it to decline; but now its numerous shops and covered arcades indicate that it is once more in a flourishing condition. The peculiar manufacture of this city is *eau de Cologne*, and we visited the most noted establishment—that of Jean Marie Farina—and purchased a box of it as a souvenir of the city; but I fear, judging from the number of times I shall have to pay duty while passing through Germany, that it will prove a dear investment before I get home. Throughout the Continent, custom-house officers are stationed at the different approaches to almost every town, who step up to your carriage in order to see if you have anything contraband. Each city seems to have some special article which they wish to prohibit. In Paris wine or spirits is the principal commodity looked for, and the duty upon it yields an immense sum—so much that it is difficult to get a pure article, the adulteration is so very great.

XIX.

AMSTERDAM: ITS EXTERNAL FEATURES, INDUSTRIES, GAL-
LERIES OF ART AND BANKING HOUSES.... HAARLEM AND
ITS FLOWER GARDENS.... LEYDEN AND THE "PILGRIM
FATHERS".... ROYAL MARRIAGE FÊTE AT THE HAGUE
.... ANTWERP: ITS CATHEDRAL AND ART TREASURES
.... BRUSSELS: ITS HOTEL DE VILLE, LACE-MAKERS AND
MILK CARRIERS ... RETURN TO PARIS.... OUR REPRE-
SENTATIVES ABROAD.

Amsterdam, Holland.

AS we approach Amsterdam the country appears flat and marshy. We see the windmills in every direction, and regale our eyes on old-fashioned Dutch houses and numerous canals, and finally on the city itself, which in some respects is one of the most interesting on the globe. It is built on wooden piles. All through the city you cross the canals, bordering which are many of the principal streets.

with long rows of shade-trees and clean, paved roadways on either side; the canals intersecting the city streets being so numerous as to form ninety islands, with two hundred and ninety bridges crossing them in different directions. Amsterdam has a population of about three hundred thousand, and is, like Frankfort, a great city for discounting and bill-broking, there being immense wealth among the Jews and many other of its inhabitants. Its style of architecture is very singular, and often strikes the stranger as angular, stiff and tasteless, the houses being constructed with curiously carved gables, which are made to front universally upon the streets.

One of the principal industries of the city is diamond-cutting, and it commands the diamond trade of the world. We visited M. Koster's diamond-cutting and polishing establishment, where four hundred workmen are employed in this, to us, interesting business. Some of the finest diamonds are obtained from the Cape of Good Hope. The famous Koh-i-noor was polished here, and it would do our ladies good to look at the little pile of diamonds which the proprietor kindly called us to examine.

Amsterdam has an academy of painting, sculpture, engraving and architecture. As regards the intellectual pursuits of its inhabitants, it is said, "No city of its size and population abounds with more societies for the cultivation of literature, science and the fine arts." At the *Felix Meritis*, lectures are delivered and dissertations read on all subjects, and it is said to be a most admirable society for the encouragement of every branch of art, science and literature, of physics, music (and they also give concerts), and even commerce and political economy.

We saw on the streets the neat, quaint costume of the girls from one of the numerous orphanages, consisting of white ruffled caps and long white aprons, and we thought that, with their ruddy cheeks, they looked both happy and pretty.

The banks of the millionaires of this city, like those of the Rothschilds and others elsewhere, were in plain old buildings, and two of them that we visited were in the back rooms of the basements of the proprietors' residences, with no sign or indication that a banking institution whose yearly transactions amounted to millions was there. We rang the bell at the front door of the dwelling, telling our Dutch driver that we were sure he had brought us to the wrong place; but he insisted upon our going in, and so we were shown into the basement by a servant. There we found one small room, which answered for the counting-room, in which were seated six or eight clerks, busy with their pens, and a private room besides, looking out upon the grounds in the back yard, where were beautiful flowers and plants.

The route to the Hague leads through Haarlem, whence for so many years we have received the bulbs which have made our gardens and grounds so rich in beauty, from hyacinths, tulips, etc., in early spring. One horticulturist exports annually three hundred thousand crocuses, one hundred thousand hyacinths and one hundred thousand ranunculuses, besides other flowers.

Ten miles from the Hague is Leyden, a place which interests us greatly, as well as Amsterdam, from its connection with the Pilgrim Fathers. It will be remembered that the English Separatists, as they were then called (now Congregationalists), were driven out of England and went to Amsterdam and Leyden in 1611, and established a church at the latter place, under the care of John Robinson, its first minister. On the spot where he then lived a large building was afterward erected, in the seventeenth century, by John Pesyn, of the Reformed Walloon Church, for the benefit of the old people of his congregation. In 1864 a monumental stone was placed on the front of the house by some American Congregationalists, with the following inscription: "On this spot lived and died John Robinson, 1611-1625."

At the Hague, one of the prettiest and pleasantest places in Holland, arches were being erected and grand preparations made in all the public squares and parks, and in front of the public buildings, palaces, private dwellings, etc., for a splendid fête on the 31st (August, 1878), in honor of the marriage of Prince Hendrek of Holland, who resides here, to Princess Maria of Prussia. The European people appear to delight in such grand displays in favor of royalty, and the expense and enthusiasm on such occasions seem unbounded. The present king of Holland is William III., and here is his chief palace. The Hague is the capital of Holland, and the two chambers of Parliament (the States General) hold their assemblies in the Binnenhof. The building is irregular, and dates back for centuries. It was here, in front of the steps, that the great Barneveldt, in 1619, laid down his head on the block, and, while he exclaimed: "Christ shall be my guide; O Lord, my Heavenly Father, receive my spirit!" at a single blow, it was severed from the body.

We obtained a carriage early to drive about the city, and noticed that in front of almost every house of prominence could be seen the clean, tidy, blonde house-girl, with her white apron and white ruffled cap and wooden shoes, scrubbing the pavement— not on her knees, however, but in a bending attitude; while everything, even to the streets themselves, was as clean as the inside of the houses. All the servant-girls in Holland seem to dress in this way. We found the market full of them, wearing on their heads only these ruffled white caps, but with no sign of a bonnet to be seen on one of them. The Dutch peasant or village girls, when you encounter them upon the road, always have a cheerful "Good-day" for you, and if you have companions they will change their greeting from "Goeden dag," in the singular, to the plural salutation of "Dag drei" if there are three, and "Dag vier" if there are four,—that is to say, "Good-day to the three of you," "Good-day to the four of you," and "Dag zamen," which means "Good-day together," if there are but two. Sometimes a roguish boy (there are such in every country) will salute a traveler who is going along with a donkey or dog with his "Dag zamen." But we must not grudge people their harmless joke.

We had the pleasure of visiting some private galleries, and the attendant took great pride in pointing out to us the cattle paintings of Paul Potter, and also pictures by Rubens, Rembrandt, etc., and, indeed, a gallery without specimens of some of the fine old Flemish masters would hardly be considered a complete one. The collection of paintings in the Royal Museum is chiefly by artists of the Dutch school. The *chef-d'œuvre* of Paul Potter, the "Young Bull," so world-renowned, is in this gallery, and the staid burghers of The Hague seem to think this to be glory enough for one city.

Antwerp, through which we pass on our way to Brussels, is the commercial capital of Belgium. It is a most interesting town, as all these Dutch towns are, with their narrow, ancient streets, where you see the Flemish peasants with their antique headgear, and everywhere around you the great old-fashioned mansions, lofty-gabled and quaint-looking enough. Here was the birthplace of several of the greatest painters of the Low Countries, notably Van Dyck, the two Teniers—and others, and all about one seems to breathe an atmosphere of art. But the Cathedral is the great place of attraction to all visitors. Its spire, four hundred and four feet high, is one of the finest we have seen in Europe, and its sculptured tracery is so exquisite "that Charles V. said it deserved to be kept in a glass case"; while Napoleon compared it to Mechlin lace. The Antwerpers are proud of the magnificent pictures that adorn the interior of this church. "The Descent from the Cross," by Rubens, is one of the noblest efforts of art in existence, and there are fourteen choice paintings beside, called the "Saints of the Passion," illustrative of the scene of the Crucifixion. Another great picture by Rubens, "The Assumption," was said to have been painted in sixteen days at the rate of a hundred florins a day, that being his fixed price for work—a somewhat more moderate charge than lesser artists of the present day demand. There are a great many other valuable pictures here—in all, estimated at three hundred—more, perhaps, than any other church on the Continent can exhibit. How these old painters could accomplish so much is indeed a wonder.

All these quaint, beautiful towns in Holland have in their centers large and beautiful parks, which everybody, rich and poor, can easily reach. At The Hague, when I got up in the morning and looked out of the window of my room at the hotel, I saw a herd of about twenty deer quietly feeding in William's Park, a pleasure-ground adorned with villas, monuments and statues. Says a Dutch author: "The Hague has a tree, a flower and a bird for each of its sixty thousand inhabitants." There are scarcely any side-walks in Dutch and Flemish towns. The streets are narrow, and horses, vehicles and pedestrians fill up the roadway, and the hack-driver continually cracks his long whip as a warning for the foot-passengers to get out of the way. The houses are four or five stories in height, and many are extremely old-fashioned in appearance, and look, as you pass along the streets, as if they were about to topple over and fall upon you, they are so out of the perpendicular—owing, I suppose, to the foundation of piles having given way; for the ground is here so low and marshy that the houses are all built on piles driven closely together into the soil. Most of the house windows in the city are provided with little side mirrors, so hung that by means of them the inmates can see all that takes place on the streets without being seen themselves, and all the houses are so constructed that the lower portions can be hermetically closed in case of an inundation, as there is a possibility of such a catastrophe from high tides of the sea coming up the canals that permeate all the streets.

Brussels, the capital of Belgium, has lost the primitive style which so many of the other towns retain, and has become a second Paris. It possesses some very fine buildings, especially the Hotel de Ville (or City Hall), a magnificent structure. I ascended the tower and obtained a fine view of the city. This tower is one of the most splendid specimens of Gothic architecture I have seen. As in all these cities, here, also, there are large, spacious parks, with fountains and statues, the principal one of which is the great resort for the fashionable world on Sunday afternoons, when a military band plays for the entertainment of the thronging promenaders. Music is a great feature of enjoyment all over the Continent. I wish heartily that we also had some arrangement for music in front of our State House, where the people of the city could resort after the labors of the day, and enjoy themselves in the cool of the evening.

No one should visit Brussels without seeing the lace-makers. The ladies at home all know something about Brussels lace, but perhaps a little information in regard to the intricacies of its manufacture would be interesting. We saw some of the female operatives at work on a Valenciennes lace scarf, which took nine hundred little spindles or bobbins, and on a lace parasol which required seven thousand spindles, and the skill with which the workers handled them was wonderful. The women looked poor and haggard, as they bent intently over their absorbing and delicate tasks. All the beautiful little figures are wrought by hand, and each girl has her separate piece to do. Some of the young girls wore glasses, and held their work near to their eyes, as if their eyesight were already affected by their too close application. The lace-makers each receive a name from the work assigned them. The *Platteuses* are those who work the flowers separately, and the *Faiseuses de point a l'aiguille* work the figures and ground together. The *Striquese* is the worker who attaches the flowers to the ground, while the *Faneuse* works her figures by piercing holes or cutting out pieces of the ground. The spinning of the fine thread used for lace-making in the Netherlands is an operation demanding so high a degree of minute care and vigilant attention that it does not seem possible ever to supplant the hands of women by machinery. The finest of this point lace is made in damp, under-ground cellars, for its fiber is so extremely delicate that it is liable to break by contact with the air above ground. This continual working under-ground has, as might be expected, an injurious effect upon the health, so that the workers here command good prices in order to induce them to follow this branch of their occupation. The girls in the other departments, however, are allowed to take their work home and sit in the window or under the shade of the trees, or even in the parks, where we saw some of them working, and where,

MILK VENDER AT BRUSSELS.

also, they were liable to be interrupted by the gay young Belgian soldier, trying to divert their attention by his winning smiles, and sometimes not without success. It is curious to see these operatives in groups, with their lace pillows, making every species of this delicate fabric, while enjoying the fresh air and bright light away from their own darker places of abode.

Milk is carried about the city here in little carts drawn by large Newfoundland dogs, and the quaint, neat dress of the girls dealing it out, and the bright, silvery cans, incline one to stop and take a draught of the milk, which we feel sure must be both clean and creamy.

Waterloo is not far from this city, and the great crowd of English tourists to the Exposition at Paris take this famous battle-ground in their route; but I had not the same cause for interest as they, and so did not visit the locality (for in only a few days more I hope to be on the ocean, "homeward bound").

On my return to Paris I found it more beautiful and attractive than ever, and the streets and boulevards still crowded with visitors to the Exposition, from every part of Europe and the world. I visited, at the kind invitation of Mr. Bierstadt, several of the studios of prominent French artists, and one in particular, that of Miss E. J. Gardner, an American lady, a pupil of Bouguereau, who has been here twelve years and has gained a high reputation as an artist, all her paintings being quickly taken up by Goupil even before they are finished. I saw in her studio, yet unfinished, two original paintings, "The Infant Moses on the Nile," and another whose scene is taken from Whittier's poem, "Maud Muller," and which is spoken of by leading artists here and American correspondents to New York papers with high commendation. On Sunday the Exposition is crowded with working people and their families. A good-looking woman, however, one can hardly see among them, they appear so worn and haggard. On this day the English and American departments are closed. Curtains are drawn over the cases of jewelry, etc., and the machinery is stopped and covered up, and no one is seen about them except the visitors, inquiring, "What does it mean?" They are told: "Because it is Sunday; they keep Sunday in England and America, and people do not work on that day, but go to church or stay at home and rest." They think that those must be queer countries, where people do not have a holiday on Sunday, and go to the *cafés* and parks and have a good time. It is said that Americans are taking possession of Paris, and that there are thirty-five thousand here, either residing permanently, or visiting the city, or in business. Professor Jonekbloet (a resident of The Hague), who is the Commissioner from Holland to the Exposition here, and was also Commissioner to our Centennial Exposition at Philadelphia, in referring to Mr. Welsh, our Minister to the Court of St. James, spoke in the highest terms of his reputation in England, and also remarked at a public table in my presence that the United States was never better represented abroad than now, with Ministers Welsh at London, Noyes at Paris, Bayard Taylor at Berlin and Marsh at Rome, etc. His association with the commissioners from the different countries and his own personal knowledge of the men gave him an opportunity for forming an adequate judgment. Governor Noyes and Hon. John Welsh live in a style worthy of the great republic; not like kings and some foreign embassadors, of whom one would judge, from their palaces and extravagant outlay on everything that pertains to them, that the world was made for royalty and them alone, and that the poor people had nothing to do but to minister to their wants. Think of the King of Italy—poor as that country is—having half a dozen palaces as large as our new Hospital for the Insane, and costing each ten times as much. And think, also, of the numerous palaces occupied by Queen Victoria, equally expensive, and of the amount appropriated each year by the English Parliament for the Queen and her family—how enormous it is; probably several millions of dollars yearly! Mindful of these things, we feel we have been long enough in Europe, and have seen sufficient to cause us to love our own country and its institutions, and cherish them more than ever.

We could not help noticing how much less it costs to run hotels in Europe than in America. I think enough is wasted in our hotels at home to amply supply the tables here. At breakfast in the morning, you are asked if you will be at "*table d'hôte* (meaning the dinner at half-past six P. M.), and thus prepared beforehand as to the quantity required, the different dishes of meat are served at the dinner-table cut up in small pieces, and generally but just enough to go around; and if a person more than they have calculated for should come in, the waiters are obliged to go back to the cook for more. At dessert, if peaches or any other fruit were served, there would be just one for each. When you go to a hotel your first business is to engage a room, for which you pay so much a day, according to location — say from thirty-six to eighty cents a day for a single room. You think that it is cheap, and that your expenses will not be great; but when your bill is presented, which is always in writing, you have a long string of items, as follows: room, meals, attendance, soap, candles, etc., whether you use them or not; and when you leave, an army of waiters expect to be remembered. When you understand this, it is all right; but it seems odd enough to us Americans at first.

The question is often asked us in Europe, especially in Paris, "Do you have opera in America?" When answered that we do, the reply was, "We could not live without the opera." It was a surprise to us to learn that Government builds, to a large extent, the opera-houses, and furnishes a generous support to them. From a report of the Chairman of the Government Committee on the Opera, we learn that the Grand Opera House of Paris is the most costly and splendid in the world, reminding one of the fabulous palaces in the tales of the Arabian Nights. To make room for it, one hundred and forty-seven houses were demolished. Its cost was thirteen millions of dollars. This magnificent edifice, begun by the late Napoleon, was fifteen years in process of erection, and is the property of the State. A manager is appointed by the Government, who receives a subsidy of one hundred thousand dollars annually to maintain the opera. Besides this, he receives, for his own services, a salary of five thousand dollars, with one thousand dollars additional for house-rent and another thousand for carriage expenses. Expenditures for new scenery, new music and other necessary outlays are defrayed also by the State. Everybody in Paris who can afford it attends the opera, for here truly it can be enjoyed in its utmost perfection. The cost to the State of mounting the various operas, as by the report of M. Tronst, is: "La Juive," $38,000; "La Favorita," $23,000;

"William Tell," $28,000; "Hamlet," $30,000; "Les Huguenots," $34,000; "Faust," $39,000; "Don Giovanni," $38,000; "Robert le Diable," $38,000; "Le Prophete," $35,000; "L'Africain," $60,000. Then there are many other theaters, also, that are patronized and assisted by the State.

Everybody here drinks wine, and Americans readily fall into the habit, on account, as they say, of the water. The water, however, is good, and we did not hesitate to drink it freely. But Americans, no doubt, like the wine better than the water, and are glad of an excuse for indulging in it. We met a prominent clergyman from New England at dinner one day, and he and his friend had their wine. When he noticed that my friend and myself were the only ones at table that had not wine-bottles before them, he said by way of apology that the water in Paris was so miserable it made him ill; but after that we noticed that the water was good enough. Our waiters at table would hand us the wine-list, and when we declined it, would throw up their hands in surprise and say, "What! no wine, no beer, no whiskey?"

The consumption of beer and wine and absinthe

is said to be on the increase in France. From reports to the Government, the annual quantity of wine drank is thirty gallons to each inhabitant. The consumption of beer has increased threefold and other spirits fifty per cent. during the last twenty years. I do not remember to have seen a man intoxicated in Paris, and there is no drunkenness in France compared with that in England. " You never see a drunken man in France " can, however, no longer be said, and Americans who have been there within three or four years past observe a difference between what is now and what has been in this respect. Parisians account for it because of the high duty paid on wines at Paris, and the consequent manufacture of bad brandy, which has come into common use among the working classes. The close connection between alcohol and disease and vice is shown by the increase of accidental and violent deaths, of mortality generally, and likewise of crime.

XX.

Paris Workingmen.... Their Social Character... Peculiarities of Domestic Life.... National Faults and their Origin.... Sunday as a Holiday.... Musical Societies; their Popularity and Management.

Paris, France.

THE true Parisian workman, although an underpaid individual compared with his more fortunate fellows in our own country, is nevertheless a merry, light-hearted being—trusting in no providence but his own right arm, and receiving both the good and evil of this life with a strange kind of philosophy drawn from the writings of Montaigne and Voltaire, whose rules are known only to himself.

Receiving a good, sound education from the State (something beyond the primary three R's), that will aid him to become a thorough workman in his trade, or an employer of others should his industry and good fortune raise him to that position, he is able to discuss with great clearness (and often talent) questions not for the moment intimately connected with his every-day life; in fact, I have heard metaphysical subjects propounded by these *ouvriers* which, though founded perhaps on a wrong basis, made them for the moment difficult to confute.

Politics are, however, *con amore*, their great subject and *forte*, and had they but a little more stability of character and truer governors and leaders of the people, they would have long since joined with our own country in showing to the world that republicanism is alone the only true and lasting government, bringing peace and liberty in its train, and prosperity with happiness to those who own its sway.

Living with his wife or mistress in some small lodgment on the fifth or sixth story, to take stock of the furniture and belongings of the Paris workingman is not a long or intricate operation. The old wooden bedstead, covered with spotless white; an old-fashioned buffet, on which are placed with neatness a few well-thumbed books and other heirlooms, cherished with care; the plain, deal table; the simple washstand, whose accessories would shock the delicate requirements of a modern belle,—these are his possessions, not much in value, but dear by the scanty earnings of poverty and many a pleasing association; while on the snowy walls, flanked by the various necessaries of the *cuisine*, a few sketches done in crayon, the product of his youthful industry and plodding hand, and which ever remind him, as he looks upon them, of the smile that lit his mother's labor-furrowed visage as with boyish glee he bore them home—a trophy of the prize from the generous hand of the kindly *Maire.'*

An old violin completes our list, which, in its time, has oft—like Goldsmith's flute—called forth the village lads to dance, soothed and assisted by the ripple of the passing Loire; and still has it music in its ancient bosom, and in its loving master's hands yields forth many a gay and heart-touching melody.

Starting at daylight to his toil, the Parisian of the working classes labors without intermission, excepting the occasional interval demanded by the indulgence of his cigarette, until the midday meal. This is usually composed of *bouillon* (or thin soup), followed by the meat from which it is made, and after that perhaps a salad. A considerable quantity of bread is always consumed during this meal, and the whole is washed down by a *chopine* or pint of wine.

The evening repast is very similar to that of noon, occasionally varied on *fête* days by the addition of a simple dessert; while the following hours are whiled away as each one's individual taste may lead them — either in a free night-school, a concert, the theater, or in any of the current costless amusements which Paris gives her children, or even, if he so prefers, at the establishment of a *marchand de vins*, where he can play lengthy games of cards, lasting the whole evening, at the expense of a few sous.

They are not a drunken race, and it is rare (excepting, at times, on pay-day) to meet many intoxicated *ouvriers* on the streets.

Sunday is their great holiday. Then, arrayed in a variety of costumes, such as only Frenchmen wear, or in the uniform cap and blouse, they sally forth, attended by their *connaissance*, to seek in the environs of Paris fresh air and the amusements suited to their inclinations. There is one pursuit which is exceedingly popular among them, which would have delighted the heart of Ike Walton, though it might also have excited his wonder at their *modus operandi*, and that is—fishing! for, you may see them lining the banks of the Seine by hundreds, waiting with patience until it may please some unaccountably deceived member of the finny tribe to nibble at their bait; and, moreover, always good-humored, witty and polite are they to those who may wish to converse with them.

Such are the men who, in this short sketch, I have endeavored to portray to you. That their faults are many, I do not deny, but they are the result of the evil training and vile misgovernment that centuries of despotism have imposed upon them. Their virtues are their own, and will repay with pleasant experience any lover of human character who, leaving the vicious and Pinchbeck Paris life, cares for a moment to cultivate the acquaintance of her working sons.

Among the many amusements which abound in this city to allure the workman after his day's labor, none are so worthy of commendation as the societies formed for choral and instrumental music. These societies, composed of bands of young men, count from thirty to one hundred members, who elect from among themselves their secretary and treasurer, choosing generally for president and vice-president some willing citizen who possesses both a generous heart and an ear for music. The position of *Chef* (which is an onerous one and commands implicit obedience) is usually filled by some retired army band-master, or, in the case of choral societies, by a decayed public singer. They are in the custom of meeting once a week to practice in some convenient spot, which may be a commodious room in the case of the more opulent societies, or the cellar beneath a *café* with those of humbler means. The subscription paid by each member—one franc per month—is devoted to the purchase of music, paying the conductor of the band, and to other incidental expenses. Each member provides his own instrument. At length, after diligent practice during the first winter and spring months following their formation, the long-expected day arrives when, marshaled behind their virgin banner, they sally forth to some *concours*, fervently hoping that a medal will reward their diligence and trial, to reflect back the sun's setting rays on their homeward march. Several of these societies—of which there are some two hundred and fifty in Paris—have gained from forty to seventy of these medals. These are always displayed on their banner in their jovial processions, borne with harmless pride by some non-playing member, delegated for that purpose. On arriving at the *concours*, each society plays and sings in turn a selection of music before the judges, consisting of celebrated composers, who give their services on these occasions gratuitously. The various medals are then distributed according to merit, without favor or partiality, and it is worthy of record that there is never any question as to the justice of the decision. At the end of the year, a dinner and ball are given by the societies to their friends of either sex, where it would seem that Mirth, never a respecter of persons, has abandoned for the nonce the richer saloons of the great to take up her abode with the humbler followers of the sweetest of the Muses.

While in Paris, I talked with an intelligent man in my employ at the Exposition, and gathered the above facts in regard to Parisian workmen. We often hear a great deal about the higher classes of society in Paris, and but very little about the great masses of those whose daily toil is hidden in the obscurity of their lives—men who, miscalled the lower classes, are in fact the muscle and sinew of every land, and in whose honest or perverted training lies the future of their country's destiny; and so I thought that a letter about these Paris laboring men could not but prove interesting to every citizen of a country like our own.

XXI.

STRATFORD-UPON-AVON....SHAKESPEARE'S HOUSE....RELICS OF THE POET STILL EXISTING....TOMB AND EPITAPH IN THE CHURCH OF THE HOLY TRINITY.

Stratford-upon-Avon.

ON our way home from London to Liverpool we made a detour to the home of Shakespeare, at Stratford-upon-Avon, his birthplace and burial-place. The first thing that attracted our attention, on stopping at the depot, was an omnibus with a prominent sign on it, reading "Shakespeare Hotel." We must, of course, go to the Shakespeare, where they showed us a room that the poet used to lodge in, whilst they also claim that the hotel itself is over four hundred years old. We first called at an odd, antiquated-looking building, where his father was living in 1552, and where in 1564 the bard himself was born. We were cordially received by two aristocratic, intelligent-looking maiden ladies, who showed us through the apartments, pointing out the room in which he was born, where he studied and wrote several of his most matured and original dramas, where his father stored his wool (for he was a wool stapler), etc., etc., explaining minutely everything of interest in each. Much that is said about Shakespeare is legendary or imaginative; for the facts in regard to his early life have to be gathered from scanty sources. So little in reality is known of his history, that, not many years ago, a book was written by a highly cultured lady claiming him to be a myth, and that the immortal dramas attributed to him were mainly the production of Lord Bacon; and it is a well-known historical fact that of the scanty records we have of his life not all can be relied upon as absolutely trustworthy, and that such charges as that upon which he was apprehended and brought before Sir Thomas Lucy,—deer stealing,—with other trivial anecdotes more or less reflecting upon the stability of his moral poise in earlier years, have at least a doubtful origin, and must be taken with a grain of salt. That Shakespeare, like all strong and original characters, especially those of a poetic and imaginative cast, was full of wild impulse and caprice, may be reasonably supposed; but that the innate nobleness breathed throughout his works and demonstrated in the little that we actually do know of him must also have been predominant in his character from his earliest youth, is equally evident—so much so as to make us feel assured that, however eccentric he may possibly have been, nothing ignoble, mean or vicious ever stained his character or mingled with his life. His early marriage is but another proof of this. With a boy's enthusiasm he loved a woman older than himself. Tradition says she was beautiful, and we can imagine the young poet hastening with impatient footsteps through the lovely paths that led to the romantic cottage of Anne Hathaway, when love and nature and the dawning gleams of his youthful imagination were alike leading him to that happy goal of wedded life which he subsequently enjoyed, and to those higher elevations of poetic fame and success on whose utmost heights the world has forever stationed him.

In regard to that early marriage, Mary Cowden

Clarke, one of Shakespeare's most elegant commentators, thus happily writes: "From the uniformly noble way in which Shakespeare drew the wifely character, we may feel certain of the esteem as well as affection with which his own wife had inspired him. * * * The very slenderness of what is known concerning her is one tacit but significant proof of the worth of Shakespeare's wife and of the integrity of the feeling which bound him to her—for those women of whom least is heard are ofttimes the best of their sex; while the poet's silence respecting his affection witnesses its wealth by his own lines:

> 'That love is merchandiz'd, whose rich esteeming
> The owner's tongue doth publish everywhere.'"

The inhabitants of Stratford resent with jealous zeal any expression of doubt in regard to all they tell you about the poet, and say: "If there be one spot in old, historic England sanctified by past associations, it is the cottage where the poet of the world passed his youth, where he wooed and won, and encountered the struggles of early life—the

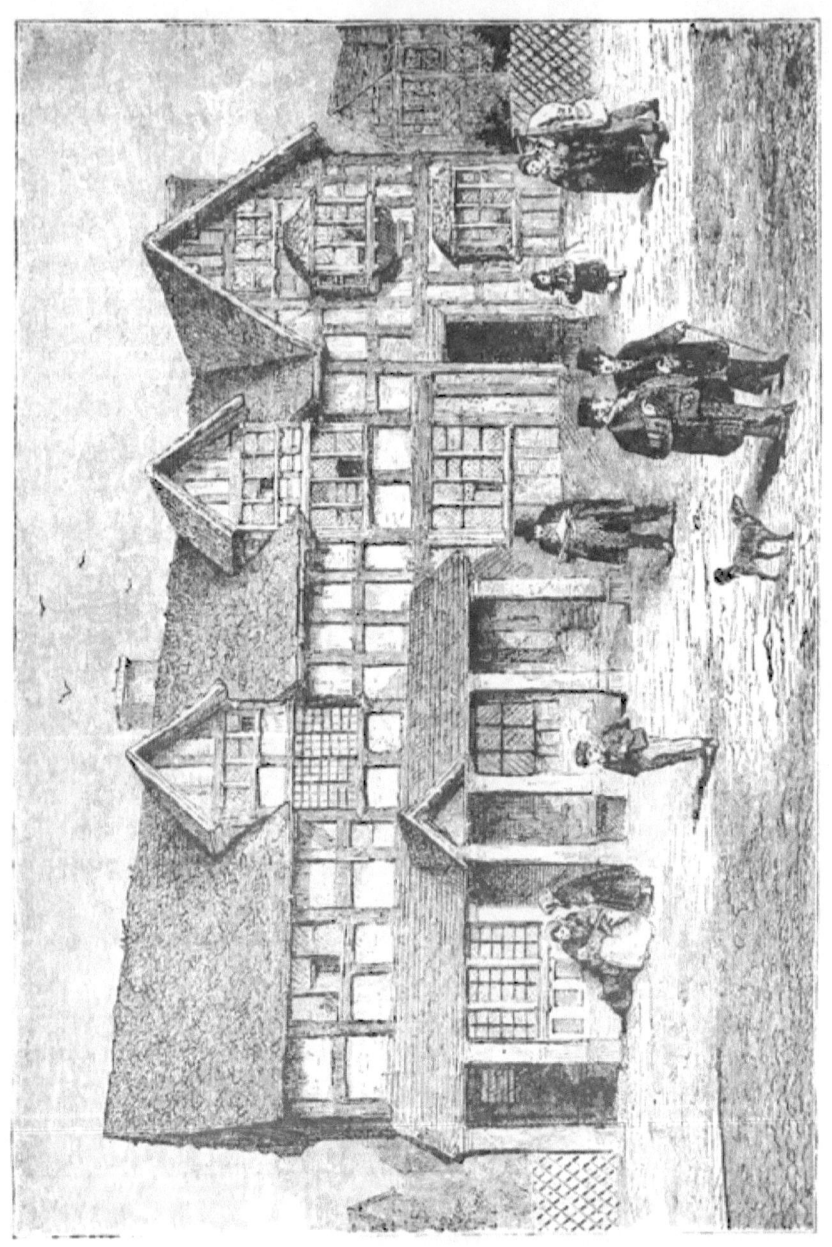

SHAKESPEARE'S BIRTHPLACE.

birthplace of William Shakespeare, who by his ripe intellectual fullness has proved himself to be a poet,

'Not for an age, but for all time.'"

No one lives in the Shakespeare house; no fire or light is permitted to be taken into it, and we noticed that it was heated by hot-water pipes coming from a neighboring tenement. To us the most interesting thing in the house, among the portraits of the bard which adorn its walls, was an old painting in oil, which has been restored, the history of which is very interesting, giving him the Saxon features instead of the dark Southern or Italian ones that we notice in all his other portraits. In this picture his hair is light and his face broad, with the good old Saxon look, and the ladies were enthusiastic in the declaration that this was the only true likeness—"it was so English it *must* be the true one."

There is not, however, sufficient evidence of the genuineness of this portrait to permit us to pronounce authoritatively in the matter. It was accidentally discovered some twenty years ago by a restorer of pictures, while on a visit from London to Stratford, who, on removing an outside coat of paint which had been applied to it by some other hand than that of the original artist, brought to view a likeness strikingly similar to the Stratford bust, and with many points of resemblance to the Droeshout print. Like most of the other well-known likenesses of the bard, it presents the lineaments of a nobly endowed man — one who must have been a shining, resplendent figure among his fellows. It exhibits the sturdy intellectual strength and physical vigor which distinguish the best of his portraits, and has qualities in common with each. The contour of the countenance, when closely examined, is found to strongly resemble the Chandos portrait and also the portrait by Cornelius Jansen, but lacks the airy grace and delicacy which distinguish that exquisite work.

The people here seem to live on the reputation which Stratford-upon-Avon enjoys as being the birthplace of Shakespeare, as thousands are thus drawn to visit the spot where one who is perhaps peerless among poets was born. A beautiful park has been laid out on the grounds where Shakespeare built his home, after the development of his wonderful genius and his great success. These grounds are very charming, stretching down toward the Avon. Nothing now remains of the house except a few foundation-stones, which are surrounded by an iron fence, showing the care with which the inhabitants preserve everything relating in any way to the poet. The one to whom the property descended having cut down some of the trees about the place, which Shakespeare himself had planted, the people became very much incensed, and so the proprietor, with true English arbitrariness, rather than be troubled with people calling to see the poet's home, and also to spite the inhabitants, tore the building down and moved away, and now, alas! only these few foundations remain to be seen. The ancient grammar-school building where he was educated still exists, and the old desks remain as in the poet's days. A school is still held there, where boys are educated, expecting, no doubt, to catch something of the genius of Shakespeare from the venerable walls and furniture.

We visited the chapel of the Guild of the Holy Cross and St. John the Baptist, where he used to worship. It was erected in 1450, and is one of the few objects in Stratford which appear now as they did to the eyes of Shakespeare. His tomb, erected under the north side of the chancel of the Church of the Holy Trinity before 1623, is noticed as you pass along between the old oaken pews, which are so curiously and grotesquely carved. We do not take much notice of anything about us, as we are wholly intent on seeing whatever may be connected with Shakespeare. We refer, of course, to the tomb of the poet himself. The grave-stones of the family lie in a row in front of the altar—that of his wife, Anne Hathaway, being situated beneath her husband's tomb, upon which are the four celebrated lines written by himself, as follows:

> "GOOD FREND FOR IESVS SAKE FORBEARE,
> TO DIGG THE DVST ENCLOASED HEARE:
> BLESTE BE YE MAN YT SPARES THES STONES,
> AND CVRST BE HE YT MOVES MY BONES."

There is a traditionary story which says: "His wife and his two daughters did earnestly desire to be laid in the same grave with him, but that not one, for fear of the curse above said, dare touch his grave-stone."

Stratford is an antiquated old English town, and

chiefly interesting from being connected with Shakespeare. Situated almost in the heart of England, and nearly equidistant from those palace-fortresses which his own writings have made grand in story — Kenilworth and Warwick — the scene of many a gorgeous pageant in the poet's life-time; surrounded by towns and battle-fields whose names the bard has rendered more glorious than history itself, Stratford-upon-Avon nevertheless is a place of sweet and rural simplicity. The curious traveler, leaving this shrine of a nation's heart, may wander at his will over the romantic sites of Naseby Field or Worcester, Edge Hill or Bosworth, or he may even visit the gray old streets of Coventry, through which the roystering Falstaff refused to lead his scarecrow phalanx, declaring, "I'll not march through Coventry with them, that's flat!" but amid all their varied points of interest, of romance or history, none will be found equal to that which nearest touches the heart and influences the mind — to the one Mecca-like shrine in the cloistered aisle of the dim old church at Stratford, where repose the sacred ashes, undisturbed forever, let us hope, of "the foremost man of all the earth."

XXII.

Conclusion: On the Atlantic.... Thoughts of Home.

AFTER leaving Stratford-upon-Avon, we were anxious to visit the splendid ruins of Kenilworth Castle, in remembrance of Sir Walter Scott's novel of "Kenilworth" and the graphic description therein of the events which transpired in that splendid medieval pile when Dudley received the visit of his sovereign, the great Elizabeth; but we had to forego that pleasure, ardently as we desired it, as our grand old steamer, the *City of Berlin*, was to leave Liverpool for New York the next day, and our passage was engaged. We passed through Birmingham on our way to Liverpool, and remained there over night. But much more time than this would be necessary in order to see the greatest manufacturing city of the world, and as our thoughts were too eagerly bent on home to be greatly interested in any other subject, we hastened on to Liverpool. On our arrival there we went at once to the office of the Inman Line, in order to look up the various boxes and packages of pictures and souvenirs which we had forwarded by express from Venice, Rome and Paris. Much to our disappointment, some of the most valuable of them could not be found, although they were forwarded by express weeks before. The business of checking baggage, which has been so thoroughly systematized by us in America, has never been adopted in Europe, and hence arise great confusion and inconvenience, trunks being thrown into the baggage-cars unchecked and simply marked with chalk, or having a paper pasted on with the name of the place of your destination; and the consequence is that when people go to look for their baggage a general scramble ensues. The system of expressing goods, also, is not so well arranged as in the United States, and cannot be relied upon for promptness and efficiency as with us. Some of our packages, in fact, did not come to us until we had been weeks at home, depriving us, therefore, of the pleasure of at once bestowing on our arrival the presents which we had purchased for friends whilst abroad.

We are glad at length to get once more into our state-rooms, which had been reserved for us, and sing "Homeward Bound." Here we met quite a number of passengers who had come over with us, and it was truly interesting to listen to some of their experiences in travel, and hear them ask if we had visited such and such a place or seen such and such a thing, and if we had not happened to enjoy that privilege, they would exclaim: Why! you have just missed the most desirable and wonderful view, or cathedral, or old ruin in all Europe; I would never return to the United States without having seen it, etc. Then, again, we meet with those whom we had encountered on the Alps or at Rome, or Naples, or on the Rhine, and it was delightful to talk over with them our various experiences, every one being so well satisfied with their tour, and quite certain that they had seen more and had had a better time than anybody else. Some had been to Russia; some had traveled through Scandinavia; and some had visited Spain or Portugal; and as *we* had been to none of these places, of course we "had missed so much." But we were satisfied that we had seen more, traveled further and packed away more knowledge for future use than any one of them! It is a wonder how much the average American can pick up during a few months of travel abroad, and how glibly he can talk about cathedrals, paintings, sculpture and the "old masters." Some marvel that one can be so much interested in old ruins, mere piles of stone overrun with vines, as they consider them, never dreaming that the interest which they hold is not their present appearance alone, but the wonderful histories with which they are often connected. Others would say: "I spent all my time viewing galleries of painting or sculpture, as there are none such to be seen in the United States." But as for myself, I have rather endeavored to observe the thousands of commoner things that came daily under my notice—the social customs, methods of business, and all the ways and doings of the peoples of the different countries that I visited, the landscapes, also, and the cities so strange and quaint, and in such vivid contrast with those of our own country. Everywhere we met Americans (especially ladies) who felt themselves free to say "that there was no culture in America." "*I* prefer," they would add, "to live in Paris or Florence, where one can gratify their æsthetic tastes"; and oftentimes you would find these very people "murdering the King's English" in their attempts at conversation, and showing in various other ways their lack of true culture and refinement. A story was related to me of one of these cultured ladies, as follows: "In Venice are some winged lions, standing here and there upon the façades of the principal buildings, and at other points, also, as imposing ornaments, or, as it is often put, St. Mark and the lions—St. Mark being the patron saint of the city and the lions being emblematical of the saint. A lady had traveled, and was again at home; some one said to her: 'And so you went to Venice? saw all the sights—St. Mark's and the lions?' 'Oh, yes, the dear old lions! we were most fortunate the day we were there; arrived just in time to see the noble creatures fed!'"

Our experience on our voyage home was about the same as on our passage over. I was often approached by passengers on board with the remark: "You are a good sailor." "Yes," I replied, "I have not been sick an hour, and have eaten a good hearty meal whenever an opportunity offered." Oh, such delightful sea-breezes one gets walking the deck by moonlight, and breathing in the salt air from old ocean, thinking meanwhile of home and friends. Each day we counted the miles that we had made, and our hearts rejoiced as we came in sight of New York; and as we steamed up through the Narrows into the beautiful harbor, it seemed as if, in all our travels, we had witnessed nothing more picturesque and lovely. As we approached the landing, all got out their opera-glasses to obtain the first glance at friends who were waiting on the pier to greet them on their return. You could hear people exclaim: "Oh, I see them! I see them!" And such a waving of handkerchiefs takes place, as in very foretaste of the joy that one experiences in meeting beloved friends face to face once more, after intervening months of absence. One and all had laid off their traveling garments, and the ladies in particular appeared in their silks and splendid suits, with cloaks of seal-skin and velvet, although it was still September. Such an array of diamonds and precious stones I never had witnessed before. The gentlemen also had on their new suits and overcoats, and a better dressed company never landed in New York. Was this all to greet friends, and appear in gorgeous array, or was it to defy the Custom House officers and say to them: "This is my apparel, and is not therefore subject to duty"? All dread the Custom House officers, and every means is resorted to in order to deceive them. Trunks are overhauled, and all having goods liable to duty either must pay that duty or submit to having their trunks sent to the Custom House. My plan was already determined upon. I showed all my goods, with their invoices, and so was the first to get a release, which enabled me to hasten at once (and with eager alacrity) to the Pennsylvania Central Railroad office for home.

If I may be pardoned, I should be glad to indulge a little local pride, and say that, in all my travels, I have not seen so prosperous and thrifty a city as my own city of Columbus, Ohio, nor, for its size, any place so attractive in public buildings of masterly design and splendid workmanship. The old State House, with its Doric style of architecture, massive and grand, is a noble structure, and if the dome were remodeled so as to render it symmetrical with the other parts of the building, surrounding it with columns, as has been suggested, it would challenge the criticism of the world. Our Hospital for the Insane is the largest of any yet erected, and all of our public buildings — the Idiot Asylum and those for the Blind, Deaf and Dumb, the Ohio State University and the Penitentiary — are certainly, considering their cost, equal, for style of architecture, to any in the world, and would attract the attention of all who are competent to judge in the matter.

THE END.

APPENDIX.

In the account of our visit to the home of Burns, given in the fifth chapter, we refer to a letter which one of his nieces had read to General Grant — a letter written by the poet to a younger brother, recommending him to cultivate a reticent spirit. This letter was subsequently copied and forwarded to us by the poet's aged and venerable nieces, and, together with their kindly and cordial letter, is appended below:

BRIDGE HOUSE, AYR, 9th February, 1880.

Dear Sir:

Yours of the 6th January arrived all right. I regret being so long in answering it, but we meet with so many interruptions, you must excuse the delay. I have now got the letter of my uncle copied, and hope the post will not put off as much time as I have done in the matter. "It is from the poet, to his younger brother William." We were glad to hear you and your friend had enjoyed your visit to Scotland; but the Americans seem all to do so, and we like them all the better for that. My sister joins in kindest regards.

Yours, most sincerely,
ISABELLA BURNS BEGG.

Copy of an unpublished letter, the previous one referred to bears date March 2d, 1789:

ISLE ELLISLAND.

Dear William:

In my last I recommended that invaluable apothem, Learn taciturnity. It is absolutely certain that nobody can know our thoughts; and yet, from a slight observation of mankind, one would not think so. What mischiefs daily arise from silly garrulity or foolish confidence! There is an excellent Scotch saying that "A man's mind is his Kingdom." It is certainly so; but how few can govern that kingdom with propriety. The serious mischiefs in Business which this Flux of language occasions do not come immediately to your situation; but in another point of view, the dignity of the man, now is the time that will either make or mar you. Yours is the time of life for laying in habits: you cannot avoid it, though you would choose; and these habits will stick to your last sand. At after periods, even at so little advance as my years, 'tis true one may still be very short-sighted to one's habitual failings and weaknesses, but to eradicate or even amend them is quite a different matter. Acquired at first by accident, they by and by begin to be as it were convenient; and in time are in a manner a necessary part of our existence. I have not time for more. Whatever you read, whatever you hear, concerning the ways and works of that strange creature man, look into the living world about you, look into yourself, for the evidence of the fact, or the application of the doctrine.

I am ever yours

ROBERT BURNS.

Addressed

MR. WILLIAM BURNS
Saddler
Longtown
England.

www.ingramcontent.com/pod-product-compliance
Lightning Source LLC
Chambersburg PA
CBHW020246240426

43672CB00006B/657